International Culinary Dictionary

Derek A. Pines

SUMMERSDALE

Summersdale Publishers
46 West Street
Chichester
West Sussex
PO19 1RP
United Kingdom

A CIP catalogue record for this book is available from the British Library.

ISBN 1 873475 63 2

Printed and bound in Great Britain by Selwood Printing Ltd.

*To my close friends who have not only encouraged me to
compile this dictionary, but endured my culinary experiments
with a multitude of new and exciting ingredients.*

Introduction

Wander around your local supermarket and you will realise that the modern consumer is thoroughly spoilt for choice. With more and more exotic products now available the range of foodstuffs is becoming truly international, with the result that cooking is now fresh, imaginative and strongly influenced by the prevalence of previously unusual ingredients.

Along with the growth of the food market, healthy eating is now an important part of many people's lifestyles. The diet industry has capitalised on this and vegetarianism is increasing in popularity.

However, even for an already confident cook this vast array can be a little awesome. This dictionary will guide you through the culinary minefield - never again need you be confused by *alfalfa* or *zabaglione*. Simply look up the word and a simple and informative description will answer your questions.

It is virtually impossible to cover everything edible and drinkable in this dictionary and precise definitions of certain culinary terms are subject to debate. I hope this book will assist everyone who has tasted the delights of foreign food and wishes to recreate that enjoyment in their own kitchen.

OVEN TEMPERATURE CHART

F	C	GAS	DESCRIPTION
225	110	1/4	VERY COOL
250	130	1/2	COOL
275	140	1	FAIRLY COOL
300	150	2	MODERATE
325	165	3	FAIRLY WARM
350	180	4	WARM
375	190	5	MODERATELY HOT
400	200	6	FAIRLY HOT
425	215	7	HOT
450	230	8	VERY HOT
500	250	9	EXTREMELY HOT

OILS AND FATS

This chart indicates which cooking oils, margarines and fats are the healthiest, i.e. those containing the smallest percentage of saturated fats.

Oil/Fat	Saturated %	Mono-unsaturated %	Poly-unsaturated %
Coconut oil	85	7	2
Butter	60	32	3
Palm oil	45	42	8
Lard	43	42	9
Beef dripping	40	49	4
Margarine, hard (vegetable oil)	37	47	12
Margarine, hard (mixed oils)	37	43	17
Margarine, soft (vegetable oil)	32	42	22
Margarine, soft (mixed oils)	30	45	19
Low-fat spread	27	38	30
Margarine, polyunsaturated	24	22	54
Ground nut oil	19	48	28
Maize oil	16	29	49
Wheatgerm oil	14	11	45
Soya bean oil	14	24	57
Olive oil	14	70	11
Sunflower seed oil	13	32	50
Safflower seed oil	10	13	72
Rape seed oil	7	64	32

METRIC EQUIVALENTS

Imperial	Approx. Metric	Exact Metric
¼ oz	5 g	7.0 g
½ oz	10 g	14.1 g
1 oz	25 g	28.3 g
2 oz	50 g	56.6 g
3 oz	75 g	84.9 g
4 oz	100 g	113.2 g
5 oz	125 g	141.5 g
6 oz	150 g	169.8 g
7 oz	175 g	198.1 g
8 oz	200 g	227.0 g
9 oz	225 g	255.3 g
10 oz	250 g	283.0 g
11 oz	275 g	311.3 g
12 oz	300 g	340.0 g
13 oz	325 g	368.3 g
14 oz	350 g	396.6 g
15 oz	375 g	424.0 g
16 oz (1 lb)	400 g	454.0 g
2 lb	1 kg	908.0 g
¼ pt	125 ml	142 ml
½ pt	250 ml	284 ml
³/₄ pt	375 ml	426 ml
1 pt	500 ml	568 ml
1 ½ pt	750 ml	852 ml
2 pt	1 litre	1.13 litre

Abbreviations:

Austria	Aus.	Italian	It.
Australia	Austr.	Japanese	Jap.
Belgium	Belg.	Polish	Pol.
British	Brit.	Russian	Russ.
Chinese	Chin.	South American	S/Amer.
Danish	Dan.	Scandanavian	Scan.
Dutch	Du.	Spanish	Sp.
French	Fr.	Switzerland	Sw.
German	Ger.	Turkish	Turk.
Greek	Gr.	United States	U.S.
Hungarian	Hung.	West Indian	W.I.
Indian	Ind.		

All capitalised words within the definitions are also cross-referenced.

Abaisse (Fr.) : A piece or sheet of pastry, rolled out to a certain thickness. Also used to describe a layer of sponge cake or biscuit.

Abalone /Awabi /Ormer : A smooth-textured snail-like shellfish, usually available dried, frozen or canned. Used extensively for flavouring - in soups, red-cooking, or mixed frying.

Abata (Fr.) : French term for Offal.

Abel-Musk : The seeds of the aromatic *Ambrette* plant, which give off a very strong flavour of Musk. Can be mixed with coffee to flavour and heighten its stimulating properties.

Abomasum : See Rennet.

Abricote : A cake or pudding masked with apricot marmalade.

Absinthe : Liqueur made from the leaves of *Wormwood.*

Abura-Age (Jap.) : Deep-fried cakes of soybean curd. Sold cling-wrapped or frozen.

Acacia : See Gum Arabic.

Acarn : See Bream.

Ac'cent (U.S.) : American term for monosodium glutonate. See M.S.G.

Aceline (Fr.) : See Perch.

Acerola : See West Indian Cherry.

Acetabula : A family of fungi, remarkable for their broad, fleshy cupola.

Acetic acid : An organic acid used to preserve or pickle foods. Also used to stop 'blacking' when using cream etc. especially when making sauces. It also forms the basis of vinegar.

Acetomol : Sour-sweet syrup made from honey and vinegar. Used to preserve fruit.

Achar : Pickled and strongly spiced fruit, vegetables or tender shoots. Generally coloured with saffron.

Achillea : A plant whose tender leaves can be added to salads.

Acid Curd : A curd produced by coagulation of casein by acids, normally lactic acid, during the process of making cheese.

Acid Ice : A mixture of whisked egg-whites, sugar and lemon juice, in the style of meringue, used to cover the tops of puddings and pies.

Acidify : To add lemon juice or vinegar to a culinary preparation.

Acidulated water : The addition of lemon juice or vinegar to cold water - which prevents discoloration of some fruits and vegetables. To every pint of water, add 1 teaspoon of lemon juice or vinegar.

Ackee /Achee /Akee : A fruit of a West African tree, *Blighia sapida*, in honour of Captain Bligh, who introduced it to Jamaica.

Acorn : A member of the Squash family of vegetables. No connection with the unpleasant non-culinary nut of the Oak tree. See Squash.

Acorn Barnacle : Also known as Balane, Acorn Shell or Turban Shell. A small shellfish with delicate flesh and prepared like crab.

Acorn Shell : See Acorn Barnacle.

Acquette : A very aromatic liqueur.

Actinia : (Starfish). A sea anemone with a similar flavour to crab.

Admiral : A hot punch made from claret, sugar and spices, and thickened with egg yolk.

Adoc : A name sometimes given to sour milk.

Advocaat : A Dutch liqueur made from brandy and fresh egg yolks.

Adzuki /Aduki /Azuki Beans (Jap.) : Small reddish-brown Japanese beans often used in sweet dishes, but are mainly used for growing Bean Sprouts. The short white sprouts have a crisp, nutty flavour, which can be eaten raw in salads or as an ingredient in many Oriental dishes. The beans are available dried or cooked in cans.

Aemone (Jap.) : Salad.

Aerated Bread : A mass production bread made without yeast, but with mechanically induced carbon dioxide. More easily digested than yeast or balm bread.

Aerated Flour : Another name for Self-raising flour.

Aerated Water : Water that has been either naturally, or artificially charged with carbonic acid gas, such as spring water or soda water.

African Horned Cucumber : See Kiwano.

Agami : A South American bird used mainly in consommés, or braised with rice.

Agar-Agar : (Macassar Gum, Gelose, Isinglass or Vegetable Gelatine). Dried purified stems of seaweed usually comes in thin strips, powder or flakes, which **must** be soaked before use, which then swell and form a gel. It is used as a thickening agent in soups, jellies, ice cream and pastas. Can be used as a substitute for unflavoured gelatine. Particularly useful for vegetarians.

Agaric Orange : See Orange Agaric.

Ageing : Also known as 'Improving'. Normally refers to storing flours or wines to improve the quality. For Meat, See 'Conditioning'.

Agemono (Jap.) : Deep-fat- fried food.

Agi /Aji : A small dwarf pepper of the capsicum family.

Agnolotti (It.) : Small parcels of forcemeat in a noodle paste and poached.

Agone D'istra : A small fish with the same taste as sardines.

Agou : A small brownish-grey grain which is cooked as rice.

Agras : Granulated almond milk made from almonds and verjuice. Normally mixed with Kirsch as a drink.

Aguaxima : A species of Brazilian pepper.

Aguneate : (Palta). A green calabash-shaped fruit with an insipid flesh the texture of avocado.

Aiguillettes : Cookery needles, or thin strips of cooked fish or meat.

Aillade (Fr.) : Used to describe preparations dominated by garlic.

Aitch Bone : (Edge Bone). The cut of beef lying just over the rump. Also known as 'Poor Man's Sirloin'

Aji-No-Moto (Jap.) : See M.S.G.

Ajoutees : Used to describe preparations that are mixed or added, such as garnishes or side dishes added to, or served with a main course.

Ajowan /Ajwain (Ind.) : (Bishops Weed). From the same family as parsley and cummin, the seeds of which contain thymol oil, and thus has the same flavour as, and can be substituted by thyme. Used in many Indian lentil dishes.

Ajwain (Ind.) : See Ajowan.

Akee : see Ackee.

Ala : see Bulgar.

A la Carte : Bill of fare from which the diner selects individual dishes, or dishes cooked to order. See also Table d'Hôte.

A la crème (Fr.) : Served with cream or a cream-based sauce.

A la mode de (Fr.) : In the style or fashion of.

A l'anglaise (Fr.) : In the English style, e.g., boiled and served without a sauce.

Alaria : A genus of seaweed, the most common varieties being the badderlocks and murlins, where only the sweet, central vein is eaten.

Albacore : A species of tuna fish.

Albarelle : A species of edible fungi which grows on chestnut trees and white poplar.

Albedo : (Mescarp) The white pith from the inner skin of citrus fruits.

Albigeoise : A meat garnish made of stuffed tomatoes and potato croquettes.

Alboni : A well flavoured brown sauce made from red currant jelly and roasted beech nuts, and normally served with venison.

Albumen : Egg-white. Used as a source of pectin in commercial use.

Al Dente (It.) : The cooked texture of pasta or rice, being firm to the bite.

Alectryon Fruit : Red coloured fruit with a pleasant acid taste used mainly in beverages.

Alevin : The first stage of a salmon.

Alfalfa : A legume whose very small seeds make excellent home-made bean sprouts, for use as an ingredient in salads and sandwiches. The seeds have a nutty, sweet pea-like flavour, which are often used to sprinkle over breads, cakes, pastries and desserts. Rich in minerals and vitamin B.

Alicante : A popular, rather sweet, red dessert wine from Levante.

Alimentary Paste : Shaped, dried dough made from semolina or wheat flour and water, and sometimes with eggs and milk. Commonly known as pasta. The dough is partly dried in hot air first, then more slowly.

Alla (It.) : In the style of, e.g. Alla Parmigiano, meaning ' in Parmesan style'.

Allemande : A well reduced white velouté sauce.

Alliaria : A plant whose garlic flavoured leaves are used as a condiment in salads.

Alligator Pear : See Avocado Pear.

All-Purpose Flour : A common flour, which is available in two main forms for different uses. See Plain flour and Strong flour.

Allspice : (Jamaican Peppers or Pimento). They are the dried unripe berries of the *Pimento* tree, containing a volatile oil, which gives an aroma of nutmeg, cinnamon and cloves. A versatile spice, available whole or powdered, and used in many recipes from soups and meats, cakes and puddings to liqueurs and chocolate.

Almond : Small, oval, flat nuts in lightbrown hard, pitted shells, which vary in flavour from bitter to sweet. Can be bought shelled or unshelled, but are always best when purchased in their thin brown skins, which can easily be removed by blanching for a few minutes. The bitter variety are best roasted, and used mainly in jam making, whilst the sweet variety can be added to anything from salads to stuffings or desserts.

Almond Paste : (Marzipan). A mixture of 25% ground almond, and 75% sugar.

Almonds-Earth : Small almond-shaped tubers with white starchy flesh eaten raw, or cooked as chestnuts.

Alocasia : A West Indian plant whose voluminous rhizomes are cooked as a vegetable.

Aloe : An extract from the leaves of the *Aloe* plant, which is similar to glycerine, and is popular in Africa for medicinal purposes.

Aloo : See Potato.

Aloumère : A variety of garlic with a sweetish taste. Prepared as mushrooms.

Alpheus : A crustacean resembling a crayfish, and prepared as a lobster.

Alsacienne : Dishes whose main ingredient is sauerkraut.

Alstroemeria : A root tuber, the most common of which is used to produce arrowroot.

Altitude : Affects cooking times and temperatures, where the higher the altitude, the lower the temperature is required to boil water.

Alum : A white transparent astringent mineral salt, commonly used to whiten flour.

Amandine (Fr.) : Cooking or coating food with almonds.

Amaranth : A plant whose tender leaves are cooked as spinach.

Amaretti (It.) : Sweet, almond based pudding biscuits

Amaretto (It.) : Almond based liqueur

Amazu (Jap.) : Sweet vinegar sauce.

Amchoor /Amchur (Ind.) : Dried slices of unripe green mango, usually available in powdered form. Used as an acidic, souring and flavouring agent in Indian vegetarian curries. Can be used as a substitute for tamarind.

Ameaux : Pastry made from puff paste and eggs.

American Cress : See Land Cress.

American Partridge : A common partridge in America, larger than a quail.

American Rice : See Bulgar.

American Yam : See Sweet Potato.

Amino Acids : An important group of acids for the health and efficient functioning of our bodies, of which there are 8 essential acids, and 12 not so essential ones, which are required by the body through food to produce proteins.

Amiral : Fish dishes garnished with mussels, oysters and mushrooms.

Ammocoete : Fish similar to the eel or lamprey.

Amomum : A globular pod of the ginger family. Used as a substitute for cardamom or pepper.

Amontillado : A popular medium sherry, best when served slightly chilled.

Amopendrix : A small variety of European partridge.

Amourettes (Fr.) : A culinary term for the spinal bone marrow of oxen, sheep and calves, poached, seasoned and served as a garnish.

Amulet : An old name for a sweet omelette.

Amuse-goûles (Fr.) : appetisers

Amygdaline : A term applied to all preparations that contain almonds.

Anago (Jap.) : Sea-eel.

Anardana : See Pomegranate Seed.

Anchovy : A small herring-like fish, normally sold prepared, in a marinade with a high 12% salt content producing a strong salty flavour. Used to garnish savoury dishes such as pizzas.

Anchusa : See Bugloss.

Ancienne : A term describing braised dishes involving mixed garnishes.

Andalouse : A variety of cold dishes prepared with tomatoes, mayonnaise, sweet pimentos, chipolatas, aubergines and rice pilau.

Andouille : A large sausage composed of chitterlings and stomach of the pig. Generally served cold.

Andropogon : A variety of Blue Grass, whose main species is sugar cane.

Anethum : See Fennel

Angel Fish : See Monkfish

Angelica (Fr.) : A herb whose processed, bright green, crystallised stems are used to colour, flavour and decorate cakes and confectionary. The extracts from the roots are used in the production of liqueurs, including vermouth.

Anglaise : A mixture of eggs, oil, salt and pepper, to form a batter used to coat food before dipping in bread crumbs and frying.

Angler : (Dog-fish, Frog-fish). A large ugly, rather tasteless but meaty fish often used in bouillabaisse.

Angostura : A brand of aromatic bitters made from the bark of the *Galipea Cusparis* tree. Used in certain drink cocktails and fruit salad recipes as required. Use sparingly.

Animelles : Culinary term for animals testicles.

Aniseed : (Sweet Cummin). A ground spice with a distinctive liquorice flavour, derived from an essential oil known as anethole, which is also present in star-anise and fennel.

Anise-Star : See Star Anise.

Annatto : A yellow colouring, often used to tinge butter and cheeses.

Anon : A variety of Haddock.

Anona : (Purple Apple). A fruit whose colour and shape resemble an artichoke. The flesh is cream coloured, sweet and strongly scented. Normally eaten raw.

Antilles Cherry : See West Indian Cherry.

Antipasto (It.) : Cold or hot Italian hors-d'oeuvre. Literally means 'Before the meal'.

Aoudzé : A strongly spiced sauce made from pimento, ginger, cloves and thyme.

Aperitif : A term used to describe any type of short drink served and taken before a meal.

A point (Fr.) : Of meat, medium cooked.

Appetiser : A term used to describe tasty savoury morsels of food, normally smaller than hors-d'oeuvres served before a meal to activate the taste buds.

Apple : A most popular fruit having some 2,000 varieties ranging from very sweet to very tart, for dessert to be eaten whole, or chopped and used as an ingredient in salads, or a normally green-skinned type known as cooking apples, which are used for stewing, baking, or pureeing. By using the numerous varieties available, with their different seasons, dessert apples are available all year round.

Apple Cucumber : An unusual type of cucumber, which is small, round and yellow, with outstanding flavour and juicy flesh. The common variety available is crystal apple.

Apple Jack (U.S.) : (Calvados). American name for Apple Brandy or Cider.

Apricots : Small stone fruits with yellow, juicy sweet tangy flesh, available fresh or dried. Fresh fruit should be firm with no bruised, squashy or browned skins. High in potassium and iron.

Apron : A small fish with succulent flesh resembling perch. Cook as perch.

Aquavit : Scandanavian spirit flavoured with caraway seeds.

Aqua Vitae : The Latin term for distilled spirit.

Arame : A mild tasting sea vegetable which is rich in iron.

Arapede : A univalve shellfish prepared as cockles.

Arborio (It.) : (Italian Rice). A variety of short-grain rice used extensively in Italian cookery. Although the grains swell, and absorb a lot of liquid, and cling together unlike long-grain rice, they do not produce a sticky mass like most other short-grain varieties. Ideal for risottos.

Arbroath Smokies : Small whole haddock smoked to a brown colour.

Arbutus Berry : (Bear Berry). Resembling a strawberry. The fruit of the *Cane Apple* shrub. Used mainly for producing wines and liqueurs.

Arca : A bivalve mollusc eaten raw, or prepared as mussels.

Archil : A bluish-red paste made from lichen. Used for colouring purposes.

Argenteuil : Highly prized variety of asparagus grown in that region.

Armagnac : A type of dry French brandy.

Aromates : Any aromatic herbs used in the flavouring of food preparations.

Aromatic Ginger : See Galangal Lesser.

Arrope : Unfermented grape juice reduced to the consistency of syrup, used as a sweetening agent in fruit desserts and wine making.

Arrowroot Powder : A white powder, made from the root or tuber of a West Indian plant, used as a thickening agent in liquids such as sauces or soups. Can be substituted by cornflour.

Artichoke - Chinese : See Chinese Artichoke.

Artichoke - Globe : It is in fact, the leafy flower head of the plant, and the edible parts being the fleshy base of each leaf, and the fond, which is the heart, exposed when the leaves have been removed, and is the tastiest part of this vegetable.

Artichoke - Jerusalem : (Winter Artichoke). The edible tuber of the plant, having either a white or purple thin skin, and consisting of a crisp, white sweet flesh. Can be boiled, steamed or deep-fried.

Artocarpus : See Bread Fruit.

Asafoetida (Ind.) : (Hing). Used in minute quantities in Indian cooking to reduce flatulence. It is obtained from the resinous gum of a plant grown in Iran and Afghanistan.

Asparagus : The young fleshy shoots of the plant, that have a unique and exquisite flavour, for which there is no real substitute. Can be served hot or cold, or included as an ingredient to enhance many dishes requiring a delicate flavour.

Asparagus Pea : (Winged Pea). Although commonly known as a variety of pea, it is in fact a vetch, which produces curiously shaped winged pods, which must be gathered while they are still small, or they become fibrous and stringy. The small pods are cooked and eaten whole like mangetout.

Aspic Jelly : Savoury clear jelly used for setting and garnishing savoury dishes. Made from the cooked juices of meat, chicken or fish.

Astrachan : A variety of caviar.

Astragal : A plant whose pods are pickled like capers, or used in cookery as required.

Astroderme : Sea fish normally used as an ingredient for bouillabaisse.

Athérine : Small fish with a delicate flavour. Commonly known as Silverside or sand-smelt. Usually deep-fried or cooked as small bass.

Atriplex : (Garden Orach). A species of spinach.

Atta (Ind.) : Fine wholemeal flour used in making Indian flat breads.

Aubergine : (Egg-Plant). Generally, a longish purple-black skinned vegetable, although less common varieties have white, yellow or green skins. All have a semi-firm white flesh and can be either stuffed whole, cubed for use in stews etc., sliced for frying or roasting, while small ones can be used for pickling. Large varieties should be sliced in half, sprinkled with salt, left for 15 to 20 minutes and then rinsed, to remove the bitter juices of this vegetable.

Au Beurre (Fr.) : Food cooked in butter.

Au Blanc (Fr.) : Food cooked in white sauce.

Aublet : Small river fish of the carp family.

Au Bleu (Fr.) : Blue; fish being cooked immediately after being caught will turn blue. Or fish cooked in salted water seasoned with vinegar, herbs and thinly sliced vegetables.

Au Four (Fr.) : Food baked in the oven.

Au Gras (Fr.) : Meat dishes dressed with rich gravy or sauces.

Au Gratin : Describes a dish which has been coated with sauce, sprinkled with breadcrumbs or cheese and finished by browning under the grill or in the oven. The low-sided dishes in which these are done are called 'gratin dishes'.

Au Jus (Fr.) : Meat or poultry dishes served with a gravy made from their own juices.

Autrichienne : Term used to describe dishes seasoned with paprika, such as goulash.

Avocado Pear : (Alligator Pear). A pear-shaped vegetable with either a hard, smooth bright-green skin, or a rough dark green skin (depending on country of origin), which should be able to be slightly depressed when ripe and becoming slightly patchy. The yellow-green flesh is ideal for adding to salads or sauces or as a starter and is the main ingredient. It has a distinctive, subtle flavour. Coat with lemon juice after preparation to prevent discoloration.

Avocet : Wading bird about the size of a pigeon with delicate flesh. Prepare as teal.

Ayapana : Leaves with a pleasant aroma as infusions in drinks.

Ayshire Cheese : This Scottish cheese has a soft and creamy texture, with a nutty, slightly salty flavour. It is perfect as a table cheese, served with oatcakes or crispbread and butter.

Azarole : The fruit of the Medlar shrub, akin to apple used in confectionary and jams.

Azi /Azy : A French term for rennet.

Azukian (Jap.) : A paste made from adzuki beans.

Azuki Beans (Jap.) : See Adzuki Beans.

Azymous : A term used to describe unleavened bread.

Baba : Cake made from unleavened dough mixed with raisins, and marinated in kirsch or rum after cooking.

Babassu Oil : An edible oil made from the Brazilian palm nut, similar in flavour and use to coconut oil.

Babiroussa : Similar to and prepared as wild boar.

Baby Marrows : See Courgettes.

Bacalao (S/Amer.) : See Klipfish.

Bacon : Joints of pork which have been either smoked, unsmoked, and then cured. Available sliced, or as whole joints.

Baconique (Fr.) : A name applied to dishes made exclusively from pork.

Badderlocks : See Alaria.

Badian Anise : See Star Anise.

Bagel (U.S.) : Round savoury roll, frequently served with cream cheese and smoked salmon.

Bagnes (Sw.) : A hard Swiss cheese, normally toasted and served with slices of rye bread.

Bag pudding : Any type of suet pudding that is wrapped in a cloth before boiling, instead of placing it in a basin.

Bagration : A cold mayonnaise sauce which contains caviar and anchovy purée.

Bain Marie (Fr.): A large pan of hot water, or 'bath', in which a smaller pan is placed for cooking contents or keeping food warm. Also a double saucepan with water in the lower half. Mainly used to cook, or keep hot, sauces, baked custards or egg dishes without the overheating that makes them curdle.

Bajet : A species of oyster whose flesh is not very delicate.

Bake Blind : To bake a flan, pie or pastry case without its filling. Prick base and fill with ceramic beads or pulses.

Baked Beans : Tinned haricot beans, normally in a tomato sauce. See Haricot Beans.

Baker's Cheese /Hoop Cheese : Similar to cottage cheese, but is not washed, but instead drained in a bag, which gives a finer grain. It contains more water and acid than cottage cheese.

Baking : A method of cooking in the oven using dry heat.

Baking Powder : (Raising Powder). A raising agent, consisting of an acid and an alkali, which react together to produce carbon dioxide, which expands during baking to make bread, cakes and pastry swell and rise. Can be substituted by a mixture of 3 parts bicarbonate of soda to 2 parts cream of tartar (tartaric acid).

Balachan : An Eastern seasoning made from ground shrimps and salt, then sun-dried.

Balane : See Acorn Barnacle.

Balaou (Fr.) : A small fish similar to sardines.

Ballotine : Joint of meat that has been boned, stuffed and rolled.

Balm : A term used to describe aromatic plants of the mint variety.

Balmain Bug (Austr.) : A variety of lobster found in Australia.

Balsam : A plant whose tender leaves are prepared as sorrel.

Balsamic Vinegar (It.) : A strong, densely flavoured vinegar, reddish-brown in colour is matured for about ten years in wooden casks made from oak, chestnut, mulberry or juniper. An expensive ingredient used sparingly in salads and sauces.

Balsam Pear : See Bitter Melon.

Bambelle : A small fish of the carp variety.

Bamboo Shoots : Crunchy, ivory-coloured shoots of bamboo, usually cut as they emerge from the ground. They have a texture similar to many root vegetables, and add sweetness and delicacy to a mixed vegetable dish. Can be purchased fresh in season. Canned shoots should be well rinsed before use, and may be stored in a bowl of fresh water in the refrigerator, changing water daily, for up to ten days.

Bamies : See Okra.

Bamya : See Okra.

Banana : A sweet-tasting fruit available all-year round. Look for firm, evenly yellowed skins with no blackened patches. Can be eaten raw on their own, or chopped and added to a fruit salad, baked, fried, flambéed with liqueurs, or added to pies, cakes, desserts, icecreams, and even breads. When prepared in advance, sprinkle with a little lemon juice to prevent discoloration.

Banana False : (Ensete). A small variety of banana which contains seeds, and must be cooked before eating.

Banana Figs : Sliced bananas that have been sun-dried, which produces this dark sticky 'fruit'.

Bancha (Jap.) : Course green tea.

Bangi : Pleasant green-coloured fruit the size of an orange.

Banh Trang Rice Papers (Jap.) : Semi-transparent, brittle round sheets, which soften in cold water and are used as edible wrappers.

Banilles : Small tapering pods similar to vanilla, with a very sugary, fragrant juice used in the manufacture of chocolate. Can be substituted by vanilla.

Bannock : Flat, round cakes made from oat, rye or barley meal.

Banon Cheese (Fr.) : A pungent-tasting cheese, originally only made from goats milk, but is now mixed with, and sometimes made exclusively from cows milk. Check label before purchase.

Banquière (Fr.) : Garnish of quenelles, mushrooms and truffles, used for chicken dishes or vol-au-vents.

Bantam : Small variety of chicken with very delicate flesh.

Baobab : (Monkey-bread). A fruit with very sweet flesh and a slightly acid flavour.

Bap : A soft, white, flat, floury Scottish roll.

Bar : See Bass.

Barbados Cherry : See West Indian Cherry.

Barbarea : See Winter Cress.

Barbarin : A fish of the mullet variety.

Barbarine : An elongated, plain yellow variety of marrow.

Barbecue : Method of cooking food over charcoal.

Barbel : A very bony freshwater fish with roes. Cook as catfish.

Barberon (Fr.) : French term for salsify.

Barberry : Green berry pickled like capers, or red when ripe, and used to make syrup or jam.

Barboteur (Fr.) : French name for duck.

Barding : Covering lean meat, game or poultry with thin slices of pork fat or bacon to prevent the flesh from drying out during roasting, or long slow cooking. See Larding.

Barley : A cereal often used to thicken soups and stews. Cooked on its own, it will make a pleasant alternative to potatoes, rice or pasta. See also Pearl Barley and Pot Barley.

Barley Flakes : Made from the whole grains, which are processed and dried. They can be eaten raw in muesli, or cooked to make a variety of porridge.

Barlichow (Ind.) : A delicious fairly hot Indian pickle made from ground prawns, herbs and spices.

Barm : An alternative for yeast or leaven.

Barnacle : Mollusc with hard flesh. Eaten raw or cooked as mussels.

Baron : Large joint of beef, mutton or lamb, made from a double sirloin joined at the backbone.

Barquettes : Oval-shaped short pastry tartlet shells, baked empty in small shaped tins, then filled with either sweet or savoury mixtures.

Barrel : A liquid measure of 36 gallons.

Basella : An edible plant prepared as spinach.

Basil : The incomparable herb for tomato dishes. Also popular in salads, sauces, soups, and with oily fish, roast lamb, chicken, duck and goose. A very versatile herb, which combines well with garlic. It is the main ingredient of Pesto.

Basmati Rice : Generally recognised as the finest variety of long-grain rice from the foothills of the Himalayas.

Bass (Sea Bass) : (Salmon Bass, White Salmon, Bar, Sea Dace, Sea Perch or Sea Wolf). It has lean white flesh, and can be either poached or baked whole, or the steaks or small fish grilled or barbecued. The delicate flesh should be uniformly pink and sweet-smelling when purchased. Can be used as salmon.

Basting : Moistening meat or poultry with the hot pan juices during roasting by pouring them over the food, using a spoon or bulb baster.

Bastion : Cold dishes, normally fish laid in aspic.

Bat (Fr.) : Culinary term for the tails of fish.

Bâtarde (Fr.) : See Butter Sauce.

Batata (S/Amer.) : See Sweet Potato.

Bath Chap : The cheek and jowlbones of a pig that have been salted and smoked.

Batter : A mixture of flour, salt, eggs, milk or other liquid, the proportions of which vary depending on the consistency required. It provides a basic part of many varied dishes.

Bay Leaves : The leaves of the *Sweet Bay*, an evergreen laurel-like shrub, grown in warm climates, and used as a flavouring for soups, rice, casseroles, curries and many fish dishes, giving a pleasant aroma. Can also be threaded onto skewers containing meat or fish. It is also a main ingredient in many bouquet garnis. The berries are used in the herbal spirit Fioravanti.

Bean : A very general term which technically covers both fresh and dried varieties of the seeds and / or pods of all leguminous plants, but to simplify this complex group, it is easier to describe the dried varieties such as soya, pinto, haricot and aduki beans as legumes or pulses, and the fresh green vegetables such as runner, French haricot and broad beans that are normally cooked and eaten in their pods, as green beans. See legumes.

Bean Curd : A smooth, cream-coloured purée of soya beans, which is highly nutritious and rich in protein, and used extensively in Chinese cooking as a vegetable. Itself is bland, but it is extremely useful in absorbing and harmonising the flavour of other ingredients, whether meat, seafoods or vegetables. Available either fresh (sold in cakes), canned, or dried. It is best when soft in texture and delicate in taste, but will only last a few days, even when refrigerated.

Bean Curd Cheese : (Tofu) Made from a puree of soya beans. Comes in small red or cream-coloured cakes. Salty and highly savoury. Like chilli oil or powder, you should adjust the quantity in a recipe to suit your own taste. Use as a flavourer in cooking or to eat with bland foods (congee or rice-porridge). Can be sold in cans or jars.

Bean Jam Or Sweetened Bean Paste : Brownish-black paste, normally used in desserts as a filling or spread. Can be substituted by chopped or mashed dates.

Bean Paste (Chin.) : A salty brown paste, made from fermented and processed soy beans, which can be used instead of soya sauce wherever a thicker sauce is required. Sold canned or in jars. See Hoisin Sauce.

Bean Sprouts : Tiny off-white shoots of mung beans (or peas). Very crunchy, can be stir-fried with most meats and vegetables. Easy to grow at home - like mustard and cress, or bought fresh. The canned types are too mushy and are not recommended. Fresh sprouts can be stored in a refrigerator for about a week, sealed in a plastic bag.

Bean Thread Vermicelli : See Cellophane Noodles.

Bear Berry : See Arbutus.

Bearnaise Sauce : Similar to Hollandaise sauce, but made with tarragon vinegar in place of white wine vinegar.

Beating : Mixing food to introduce air, to make it lighter and fluffier, using a fork, wooden spoon, hand whisk, or electric blender.

Béchamel Sauce : Thick white sauce made with savoury, flavoured milk, butter and flour.

Beche-De-Mer : (Sea-Cucumber or Sea-Slug). Comes in dried , black banana-shaped pieces, 3-6 ins. long. Must be soaked overnight. When soaked it becomes gelatinous and is usually cooked with meat or poultry.

Bedstraw : A delicate wild herb, whose stems and leaves are used like rennet, to curdle milk.

Beechwheat : See Buckwheat.

Beef : The most nourishing of all meats, and includes the flesh of oxen, heifer, cow and bull.

Beef Fillet : (Tenderloin). The undercut of sirloin and probably the most expensive cut of meat.

Beef Rump : The hindquarter joint with the sirloin removed.

Beef Sirloin : See Sirloin.

Beef Stock : A bouillon made from gently simmering meat and bone ingredients for use as required. See Stock.

Beer : A genetic term used to describe fermented malt beverages.

Beesting : See Beistyn.

Beet Leaf : See Swiss Chard.

Beetroot : A dark red root salad vegetable, which must be boiled before use. The small globe variety are sweeter and tastier, and a more pleasant shape than the long varieties. Ideal for pickling.

Beetsugar : Sucrose extracted from sugarbeet, which is identical to any other form of sucrose.

Beignets : See Fritters.

Beistyn : (Beistyn, Firstlings). The first milk produced by a cow after it has calved.

Belecan : See Dried Shrimp Paste.

Belgian Endive : See Chicory.

Belgian Salami (Belg.) : Smoked, dried and well-seasoned pork and beef salami.

Belle-Alliance : A winter pear with yellow and red skin. An excellent dessert fruit.

Bellone : A variety of large fig used for preserves.

Bel Paese Cheese (It.) : A famous Italian cheese which has an ivory colour with a thin, dark yellow rind. Soft and compact, this cheese has a delicate, slightly salty flavour. Usually served as a dessert cheese, but can be used in cooking.

Beluga : White sturgeon producing the best caviar.

Benedictine : A very sweet long established liqueur, made by the Benedictine monks. Can be used to flavour desserts, and often drunk when mixed with brandy.

Benishoga (Jap.) : Red pickled ginger.

Bergamot Orange : Variety of citric fruit whose highly scented oil and candied peel is used in confectionary, cakes and sweet dishes.

Bergkäse (Aus.) : A hard, dull yellow cheese with a dark brown rind, has a high fat content with a mild nutty flavour.

Berries : A botanical name for fruits in which seeds are embedded in pulpy tissue e.g. strawberries, grapes and tomatoes etc..

Besan Flour : See Gram Flour.

Besi : Generic term for several varieties of pear.

Beurré : Family of very juicy dessert pears.

Beurre Manie : Made from equal parts of flour and butter, kneaded together to form a paste. Used for thickening soups, stews or casseroles, and added towards the end of cooking.

Beurre Noir : Although not actually black in colour, it is a term used to describe butter that is melted and cooked to a golden brown, with a few lemon drops normally added, then poured over grilled sole or skate.

Bianco Di Spagna (It.) : A large white bean popular in Italy for soups, salads and savoury dishes.

Bicarbonate Of Soda : Often used in baking recipes as a substitute for baking powder. Also used to soften water for cooking vegetables.

Biffins : (Normandy Pippins) Peeled apples partly baked, then dried and pressed flat for future use.

Bigarde (Fr.) : See Bitter Orange.

Bigarreau : Variety of hard-fleshed cherry.

Bigos (Pol.) : A dish made from sauerkraut.

Bilberries : (Whortleberries, Huckleberries). Similar to but smaller than blueberries, and less common. Slightly acidic and suitable only for pie fillings and jams, or as a sauce condiment for red meats and game dishes.

Bile : See Gall.

Binding : Adding eggs, cream, melted fat or roux panada to a dry mixture to hold it together.

Bird's Foot Trefail : (Lotus). When dried, the leaves and stems are used to flavour marinades.

Bird's Nest : Made from the nests of sea-swallows, although not the nests themselves, but the dried gelatinous coating from inside the nest, produced by the birds. They are beige and come in three forms; small shallow cups, chips or broken cups, and porous fragments. They are sold in small boxes by weight, and must be soaked and cleaned before use. They are usually made into soup (in chicken broth) or cooked with sugar crystals and made into a sweet dish.

Biscotte : See Rusk.

Biscuit : A general term used to describe a 'snack' item of food which is basically made from a mixture of flour, fat and sugar, formed into a flattish shape, and then baked to dry out the mixture and make crisp. Also an American term for a small cake-like bun.

Bishop's Weed : See Ajowan.

Bismark Herring : Flat herring fillets pickled in spiced vinegar and onion rings.

Bisque : A thick rich soup made from shellfish.

Bitok (Russ.) : Small meat patty made from raw minced beef and bread, bound together with raw egg.

Bitter Melon : (Balsam Pear, or Karela). This gourd has an ugly, knobbly appearance, and used in vegetable curries. Its bitterness is due to a Quinine content. Available fresh or canned.

Bitter Orange : (Seville, Bigardier or Melangol Orange). Used mainly as root stock because of its resistance to citrus disease. Too bitter to eat raw, but used to make marmalade. The oil from the peel is used in the recipe for curacao.

Blachan : The commercial spelling of blacan. See Dried Shrimp Paste.

Black Beans : Sweet-tasting haricot beans, popular in the West Indies, but when salted and fermented black beans give a salty and strong taste to fish, seafoods and meat. Usually used in steaming or stir-frying in conjunction with these foods. Sold in packets or by weight. Can be substituted by French capers.

Blackberry : (Brambles). Very soft, sweet and juicy, purple to black berries of the Bramble plant, which deteriorate quickly after picking. Excellent as a fresh dessert, or for making pies, jams or jellies. See also Mulberry.

Black Bread : (Pumpernickel) Dark bread made from rye flour. See also Pumpernickel.

Black Currant : Normally sold in punnets, stripped from their stalks. They are slightly acidic in taste, and best used for pie fillings, jams and jellies. Very high in vitamin C.

Black-Eye Beans : Attractive in looks and taste, these beans are a creamy white with a black or dark yellow 'eye' or spot. They cook more quickly than most pulses and can be used as a substitute for haricot or butter beans.

Black Gram : See Urd Bean.

Black Hamburg : See Frankental.

Black Jack : See Caramel.

Black Onion Seeds : (Kalonji). Small tear-shaped onion seeds used to add piquancy to vegetables and Indian breads.

Black Peppercorns : Contribute aroma and flavour when freshly ground; pre-ground, they add only heat.

Black Pudding : A dark sausage made from pig's blood, suet, breadcrumbs and oatmeal. Normally served sliced.

Black Sugar : An unrefined sticky sugar, normally sold in health food stores.

Blanching : Boiling briefly to whiten meats and remove strong or bitter tastes from vegetables by bringing to the boil from cold water and draining before further cooking. Green vegetables should be put into boiling water and cooked for up to 1 minute. Will set the colour of food and kill enzymes prior to freezing. Also used to loosen the skins from nuts, fruit and vegetables. See Scalding.

Blancmange : Smooth, white almond-flavoured dessert jelly, made with arrowroot or cornflour and milk. See also jaunemange.

Blanket : See Tripe.

Blanquette : Veal, lamb, poultry or rabbit stew, enriched with a cream and egg yolk sauce.

Blending : Combining ingredients with a spoon, beater or liquidiser to achieve a uniform mixture. An electric blender is ideal for pureeing, grinding dry ingredients such as herbs and spices, and for making fresh breadcrumbs.

Bletting : See Softening.

Bleu : A method of cooking fish, mainly trout, by plunging them immediately after killing into boiling court-bouillon which turns the skin blue.

Bleu D'auvergne /De Salers Cheese (Fr.) : A blue cheese made from a mixture of goat's, ewe's and cow's milk. The same size and shape as Roquefort, but with a less delicate flavour.

Bleu De Bresse Cheese (Fr.) : A soft, creamy, dark-veined blue cheese with a rich taste, normally sold wrapped in foil and boxed. It is made from unskimmed cow's milk. When over-ripe, it becomes salty and dry.

Bleu Des Causses De L'aveyron Cheese (Fr.) : A blue cheese, less piquant than Roquefort. Made from cow's milk

Blind Bake : See Bake Blind.

Blini /Bliny (Russ.) : Pancake made of buckwheat and yeast, and traditionally served with caviar and sour cream.

Bloater : A lightly smoked, salted whole Herring. It does not keep well, and so must be grilled or fried on the day of purchase. Normally served with melted butter.

Blondir : To fry in butter, oil or fat until light brown.

Blood Heat : A temperature of 37^0c (98.4^0f). Food at this temperature feels lukewarm to the fingertips.

Blood Orange : (Malta Orange, Sanguine). It is small, with slightly rough skin, flushed with red, and has sweet, juicy red flesh, containing a fair number of pips.

Blood Sugar : See Glucose.

Blueberries : A dark blue berry available either on their stalks or ribbed. A rather sharp, acid flavour, and really only suitable for stews and jellies.

Blue Cheese : Cheese that contains an internal growth of the mould *Penicullium Roque Forti'*, e.g. Stilton, Roqueforte etc.

Blue Cheshire Cheese : A strong-flavoured blue-veined cheese, similar to Stilton.

Boar : See wild boar.

Bocal : Wide-mouthed jar or bottle for storing preserved or pickled foodstuffs.

Boiled Dressing : A mixture of sugar, flour, salt, mustard, vinegar, egg, and butter. When cold, store in refrigerator.

Boiling : Cooking in liquid at a temperature of 100^0c (212^0f). Mainly used for vegetables, rice and pasta dishes. Can also be used for reducing glazes and sauces.

Boiling Down : American term for reducing.

Boiling Fowl : A chicken that is normally more than twelve months old, it is meaty, but also fatty, and is only suitable for boiling, stewing or in casseroles.

Boletus Cepe : An edible fungi of the mushroom variety, with thick white flesh, and 'tubes' which must be removed before cooking.

Bombay Duck : Despite the name, this is not a bird, but a variety of fish that is eaten either fresh, or after being salted and cured. It is normally cut into small 1 inch pieces, deep-fried or grilled, and served as an accompaniment to rice and curry dishes, and should be nibbled in small pieces.

Bonavist Bean : See Lablab Bean.

Bone-Marrow : Soft, fatty substance found in large bones, commonly known as Marrow Bones

Boning : Removing bones from meat, poultry, game or fish, whether cooked or raw.

Bonito (Jap.) : Small member of the tuna family used in Japanese cooking.

Boops : Mediterranean brightly coloured fish. Can be fried or poached.

Borage : A herb with a flavour that resembles cucumber, and the young leaves are used to refreshen beverages or flavour salads.

Border : Culinary term for a prepared dish, shaped or moulded in the form of a ring.

Borecole : See Kale.

Boric Acid : A chemical sometimes used as a preserving agent.

Borlotti Beans : A member of the Haricot family. They are speckled beans in shades varying from cream to pink which cook to a creamy consistency. A member of the Haricot Bean family.

Boston Beans : See Haricot Beans.

Bottle Gourd : See Calabash.

Bottling : Preserving vegetables, fruit or preserves in glass jars or bottles without the need for refrigeration.

Bouchée (Fr.) : Small puff-pastry case, baked blind and filled with a savoury or sweet mixture. Should be small enough to be eaten in one mouthful, which is the literal translation.

Bouillabaisse : A favourite dish of fish cooked in white wine, oil, tomatoes, garlic and many varied herbs and spices.

Bouillon : Plain unclarified meat stock, or broth used as a basis for many soups and sauces.

Bouillon Cubes : Vegetable stock or meat extract formed into cubes, and used to enhance the flavour of many dishes. They can be dissolved in boiling water to make a simple broth or soup.

Boulette D'avesnes/De Cambrai Cheese (Fr.) : Spicy buttermilk cheese flavoured with herbs.

Bouquet Garni (Fr.) : Also known as 'A Faggot of Herbs'. Traditionally a bunch of parsley, thyme, marjoram, bayleaf, etc. tied with string; or a ready-made mixture of herbs in a muslin bag or sachet, for flavouring stews, soups, and sauces. Other herbs can be added to taste. Remove before serving. Can readily be bought in sachets.

Bourguignonne (Fr.) : In the style of burgundy, e.g. cooked with red wine and small button onions.

Boursin /Boursault Cheese (Fr.) : A triple cream cheese, which is soft, thick and flavoured with either herbs, garlic or pepper.

Box Crab : See Calappa.

Brains : Normally calves brain, which can be served fried or as part of a sauce.

Braise : To brown in hot fat and then cook slowly, in a covered pot, with vegetables and a little liquid. Used mainly for vegetables, meat or poultry which is too old or tough to roast.

Bramble : See Blackberry.

Bran : The outer layers of cereal grain which are largely removed when the grain is milled. Bran is a useful source of dietary fibre, and rich in vitamin B.

Brassica : A group or family of vegetables, normally associated with leafy green varieties such as cabbage, brussels, kale etc., but also includes turnips, swedes and khol rabi.

Brawn : A jellied meat dish made from the soft meat and ingredients of a pig's head. It has a pleasant, but acquired taste. Serve cold with salad.

Brazil Nut : Very oily nut with a sweet distinctive flavour, similar to coconut or hazelnut. They keep best when left in their three-cornered rough shells.

Bread : Usually refers to a loaf made generally from wheat or rye flour. Many variations and mixtures of cereals and additional ingredients of this basic recipe are used to provide a range of loaves.

Breadfruit : (Artocarpus). The fruit of a West Indian tree *A. Communis*. Normally eaten roasted when ripe, or chopped and boiled when green. Rich in starch. When roasted, it resembles the taste of freshly baked bread.

Bread Roast : A meat and vegetable dish made by removing the inside crumb of a loaf, and filling the resulting case with minced meat and vegetables, replacing the top and roasting.

Bread Sauce (eng) : Made from breadcrumbs and milk. Serve with roast poultry or game.

Bream (Freshwater) : Similar in appearance to and can be cooked as carp.

Bream (Sea Bream) : (Acarne, Chard, Dorade, Daurade or Pomfret). A round, bony fish with coarse scales, which must be carefully removed, and has a pink, delicate flesh. Can be poached, grilled or baked.

Bresaola : Dry cured beef fillet, eaten raw in wafer thin slices. A highly esteemed antipasto.

Breton : Cake made from layers of almond biscuit paste.

Brie Cheese (Fr.) : A large, circular, soft, pale yellow cheese, about 3 inches thick, with a delicate flavour and a slightly pinkish edible crust. A popular cheese made from cow's milk, and is best when cut from a whole cheese round.

Brignole : Variety of dried plum used in a similar way to dried apricots or prunes.

Brill : Flat sea fish similar to turbot, but smaller. When fresh, the skin is slightly slimy. It has yellow-white delicate flesh, and is suitable for baking or grilling.

Brine : Salt and water solution used for pickling and preserving. Or a mixture of salt, saltpetre, sugar and water used to preserve meat, which is normally subsequently smoked.

Brioche (Fr.) : Soft bread made of rich yeast dough, slightly sweetened.

Brisling : Young sprats. Generally available tinned in oil or tomato sauce.

Broad Bean : (English Windsor, Fava, Lima, Horse Shell or Soya Bean). A large pale-brown bean, available either fresh, canned or dried. They are usually shelled, though young pods can also be eaten if tender. Fresh beans can be eaten raw in salads, or cooked and served as a vegetable dish. Dried beans need cooking for a long period over a low heat.

Broccio Cheese (It.) : Delicate cheese made from goat or ewe milk.

Broccoli: The purple or white flowering heads of this plant are used with a short amount of stem remaining. Normally lightly boiled, this vegetable with its distinctive flavour and soft texture when cooked, is an excellent accompaniment to many meat and fish dishes. The vegetable known as Green Broccoli is in fact Calabrese.

Brochette : Skewer used for grilling chunks of meat, fish or vegetables over charcoal or under a grill or broiler.

Broiler : The name for a grill with a barred gridiron, on which food is placed to grill it under heat. See Grill and also Roasting Chicken.

Broiling (U.S.) : American term for grilling.

Broth : A soup or stock made from beef and/or bone extractives, with additional meat, vegetables and herbs added. It normally has a fairly thick consistency, and very filling. Similar to a thick soup or stew.

Browning : Searing the outer surface of meat to seal in the juices.

Brown Trout : See River Trout.

Brugnon : See Nectarine.

Brulê (Fr.) : Applied to dishes such as cream custards finished with caramelised sugar glaze.

Brunoise : Vegetables that are shredded very finely and cooked in butter or oil.

Brussel Sprouts : Small, miniature-like cabbages which are produced along a central stem which is discarded for preparation. The flavour is improved by not harvesting until after a good frost. Available frozen, but the flavour is not as good as when purchased fresh. Look for firm green sprouts, avoiding those with loose or yellowing leaves.

Brut (Fr.) : A term for describing dry wine or champagne.

Buck : See Deer.

Buckling : Whole hot-smoked salted herrings, which require no further cooking.

Buck Rabbit : Poached egg on Welsh Rarebit.

Buckwheat : (Beechwheat or Saracen Corn). Despite its name, it is not a cereal, but a member of the rhubarb family. It is available in the form of roasted grains, which are used to make porridge, or ground to make a beautifully light flour, excellent for crepes, pancakes, and Japanese noodles. The unroasted grains, which are greenish in colour are best cooked with other ingredients, as in a casserole, and is an excellent substitute for rice. (see Kasha).

Buckwheat Noodles (Chin.) : Nutty-flavoured noodles made from buckwheat.

Buglos : Common name for Anchusa, whose leaves are cooked as spinach.

Bugnes : Fritter made from dough and fried in oil.

Bulbous Chervil : A variety of chervil whose tuberous roots are cooked as Chinese artichoke.

Bulgur /Bulghur / Burghul : (Ala). Often referred to as Cracked Wheat, or American Rice, but is a much more refined version, which has been steamed and dried before being cracked. When cooked, bulgur swells to a fluffy texture similar to couscous. It can be cooked, or soaked and served raw in a salad. Can be used as an alternative to rice.

Bulk : Old term for Fibre.

Bullace : A variety of wild Damson Plum.

Bullock's Heart : See Custard Apple.

Bunch : See Scallions.

Burbot : (Cod-bourbot or Coney). A freshwater variety of cod, with long dorsal or tail fins. Prepare as cod.

Burdock : A perennial plant whose young shoots and roots are prepared and cooked as salsify.

Burnt Sugar : See Caramel.

Butter : Fatty extract of mammals milk, which is an essential ingredient in many dishes due to its richness of flavour, for which there is no real substitute. Generally available salted or unsalted, which is often preferred for cooking. See Clarified Butter.

Butter Beans : (Lima, Curry, Sugar or Madagascar Beans). These large creamy-white or pale green beans have a soft, floury texture and a smooth flavour. Available fresh, dried or canned.

Butter Cream : A mixture of butter and custard cream, or butter, sugar syrup and egg yolks.

Buttermilk : The residue left over from churning Butter, which has a distinctive but slightly acid flavour, and retains the casein of the original milk.

Butternut : Despite its name, it is a variety of the Squash vegetable family.

Butter Sauce : (Bâtarde). Made from butter, flour and salted water, thickened with egg yolk.

Butyric Acid : The acid produced by oxidation in butter, causing it to become rancid.

Byron : Reduced demiglace sauce combined with wine and fine shreds of truffles.

Cabbage : A main species of brassica, commonly known as 'greens'. A very popular, green, white or red-leaved vegetable, having many varieties, which are available during the different seasons of the year, which may be conical or round, loose-leaved or tightly packed. For individual descriptions, see under headings:- Spring, Summer, Winter, White, Savoy, and Red Cabbages.

Cabbage (Lettuce) : See Round Lettuce.

Cabbage Palm : Terminal buds of palm trees.

Cabernet : Variety of wine grape.

Caboc Cheese : A rich, soft, full-cream Scottish cheese, which is very pale, almost pure white on the inside, and is rolled in toasted oatmeal. Best eaten spread on biscuits with no butter.

Cachat Cheese (Fr.) : Made from ewes' milk and ripened in vinegar.

Caciocavalla Cheese (It.) : A hard Italian curd cheese. White/straw coloured, with a few holes, and a thin, smooth yellow rind, and has a mild, semi-sweet flavour.

Caerphilly Cheese : A moist, white cheese with a mild, slightly salty flavour.

Caffeine : A bitter tasting stimulating alkaloid substance which is present in coffee, tea, cola and soft drinks.

Caithness Cheese : A medium to strong tasting cheese which spreads and slices well. A soft yellow colour, and best when fairly young.

Cake : (Gâteau). The generic term for all items made from various types of pastry dough. However, the sweeter preparations such as flans, fruit pies, puddings and tarts are known as sweets or desserts.

Calabash : (Bottle Gourd). Fruit of the *Calabash* tree, with hard green shells and white slightly acid flesh.

Calabrese : The correct name for what is commonly known as Green Broccoli spears. True broccoli is the Purple Sprouting vegetable.

Calamandin : A citrus fruit resembling a small tangerine, with a delicate pulp and lime-like flavour.

Calamari : See Squid.

Calappa : (Box Crab). Crustacean type of crab.

Calcium : A substance found in bones, egg shells and milk. Vital for maintaining healthy teeth and bones.

Calf : Name for a young cow whose meat is known as Veal.

Callab Bean : See Lablab Bean.

Calorie : Unit of heat, which in culinary terms, refers to energy producing properties of food.

Caltropes : See Water Chestnut.

Calvados : See Apple Jack.

Camembert Cheese (Fr.) : This famous Normandy cheese is circular, soft, creamy, pale yellow in colour with a soft crust. It is made from whole cow's milk and has a much stronger taste than Brie. Do not allow to over-ripen as the taste becomes bitter.

Camomile : Bitter herb whose flower heads are used to make a tonic tea.

Campanula : Plant whose leaves and roots are used in salads.

Canadian Wine Cheddar Cheese : A moist cheese which has been matured in red wine.

Canapés (Fr.) : Appetiser consisting of small pieces of fresh or fried bread, toast or biscuits, topped with savoury mixtures.

Canbra Oil : A useful cooking oil made from rape seed.

Cancoillotte (Fr.) : Very strong cheese which must be melted before use.

Candida : A form of yeast which is nurtured or grown on carbohydrate and hydrocarbon media. High in protein and vitamin B.

Candied (Crystalised) Fruit : (Sweetmeat) Whole or diced fruit, which has been impregnated with crystalised sugar to make a preserved fruit delicacy. Can be eaten whole, or the diced variety can be added to dessert or cake recipes.

Candied Peel : Normally the peel of citrus fruit - particularly the Citron, which has been boiled in sugar syrup several times to produce a crystalised ingredient which is used in dessert and cake recipes.

Candle Nut : (Kemiri Nut). A hard oily nut used to flavour and thicken curries. Can be substituted with brazil nuts.

Candy : A confectionary made from boiled sugar and various flavourings. Also, the American name for sweetmeats.

Cane Sugar : A common form of sugar or sucrose, which is identical to Beet sugar.

Cannelle (Fr.) : French name for cinnamon.

Cannellini Beans : A popular bean in Italy, which combines well with tuna fish.

Cannelloni (It.) : Large macaroni tubes, stuffed with savoury fillings, topped with sauce and baked.

Canning : A method of preserving meat, fish, vegetables and fruit by placing in cans and vacuum sealing.

Cantaloupe : A variety of melon with soft juicy flesh, and an unusual biscuit-coloured 'matted' skin.

Cape Gooseberry : (Golden Berry). The fruit of Chinese Lanterns *Physalis Peruviana*, are covered by shrivelled, papery, orange-yellow husks. The plump, round, golden berries can be used as a dessert fruit, stewed or made into preserves.

Capelin : Small fish prepared as whiting.

Capellini : A fine spaghetti pasta.

Cape Peas : See Lima Beans.

Capers : Pickled flower buds of the Mediterranean *Caper* bush. Used in sauces such as tartare, vinaigrette and black pudding, and are useful additions as garnishes for salads, hors d'oeuvres and many fish dishes. See Genista.

Capon : A young and castrated cock chicken, specially bred to give a high proportion of flesh with a good flavour. Usually killed at 9 months and weighing 5-8 pounds. Excellent as a large roast.

Caponata (It.) : Sicilian dish of fish, aubergines, tomatoes, onions, capers and black olives.

Capsicum : (Sweet Pepper). A mild though still flavourful fruit of the *Capsicum Frutescens* or *Annum* varieties. Available in strong red, green or yellow colours, they are a versatile fruit, adding colour and flavour when used fresh in salads and cold dishes, or lightly cooked and added to other vegetables. Can also be stuffed and cooked with spiced meat or fish mixtures. See Chillies.

Carafe : Heavy-based bottle or flagon for holding unbottled or house wine.

Caramel : (Blackjack). A burnt sugar substance made by slowly heating sugar until a thick brown sauce is formed. Used for glazing cakes and desserts, or colouring soups, stocks and sauces.

Caraway Seed : A thin crescent-shaped seed, with a strong characteristic sweet and sharp flavour similar to aniseed or fennel used in seed cakes, cheese spreads and dips, sauerkraut, bread, biscuits, buns and sweet pickles. Do not confuse with cumin seed which is very similar in appearance and flavour.

Carbohydrates : Supply two main parts of a diet - starches and sugars, plus, when used in an unrefined state, fibre and in this state they are a very important source of energy and nutrition.

Carbonnade : A rich beef stew made with beer.

Carcase : The body or bones of an animal or fowl after having all the flesh and offal removed.

Cardamine : (Lady's Smock). A salad plant similar to watercress.

Cardamom : Dried pod from the ginger family either white, green light brown or large black varieties used to flavour many Eastern dishes, which should be slightly crushed before use to release its full flavour. Can also be purchased ground. It has a rich, sweet lemony eucalyptus flavour. The whole pod is used to flavour rice and meat dishes, and the crushed seeds for sprinkling on sweets and vegetables.

Cardinal : Variety of mullet. See mullet (Red).

Cardoon : A member of the Artichoke family, seldom found outside the Mediterranean area. It is grown for its blanched stems, which should be treated as tough, stringy celery which must be cooked before eating.

Caribbean Cabbage : An Asian plant whose roots are prepared as swedes.

Carmine : See Cochineal.

Carob Bean : (Locust Bean). The dark brown pod of a Mediterranean tree, is most commonly used ground, as a substitute for chocolate.

Carob Powder : (St. John's bread). This product consists of finely ground carob pods. Contains no caffeine and is unlikely to cause allergic reactions. Low in fat. Found in health stores.

Carotene : An important yellow substance which produces vitamins, and is present in many vegetables, butter and egg yolks.

Carp : A round, oily, freshwater fish. The best varieties are Mirror or King Carp. They can have a muddy smell and taste, and should be steeped in salted water for at least 3 hours before cooking. Can be baked or braised. See bream.

Carpion : Variety of Trout.

Carrageen : (Irish Moss). A nutritious edible seaweed, found along Ireland's rocky Atlantic coast. It is used either as a vegetable or to set jellies. See Agar-Agar.

Carre de l'est Cheese (Fr.) : A square, soft cheese, with a high fat content. It is similar to Camembert but with a milder flavour.

Carrots : These orange-red root vegetables are among the most nourishing and inexpensive vegetables. Young and slender carrots are usually sold in bunches with the foliage intact, and need only to be washed before use. Maincrop varieties are larger and coarser, and normally sold loose, by weight, and should be lightly scraped. Can be eaten raw with dips or in a salad, or cooked, and served as a separate vegetable, or as an ingredient in stews, casseroles and curries etc.

Carving : The cutting of meat joints, poultry, game or whole fish into economical and well presented portions.

Casaba : A large green skinned variety of melon.

Casein : Basically, the protein portion of milk, which is precipitated by lactic acid, or renin, and so solidifies to form products such as cottage cheese and yoghurt.

Cashew Nut : A sweet kidney-shaped nut. Normally purchased shelled, either raw or salted. An excellent addition to salads, and mild curry dishes, especially after roasting.

Cassata : Neapolitan ice cream made from mousse.

Cassava : (Manioc). A tuber from the *Manioc* plant. It is a staple food in tropical countries, but it is very low in protein. The plant roots are used to produce Tapioca.

Casserole (Fr.) : Cooking pot with lid, made of ovenproof or flameproof material. Also, a dish of meat, fish or vegetables, cooked slowly an oven or cooker.

Cassia : See Cinnamon.

Cassina : A beverage similar to tea, made from the cured leaves of the Holly bush.

Cassoulet (Fr.) : Stew of haricot beans, pork, lamb, goose or duck, sausages, vegetables and herbs.

Castagnaci (It.) : Thick fritter or waffle made from chestnut flour.

Castor Oil : Seldom used in cooking. The oil from the ricinus bean, mainly used as a purgative.

Castor Sugar : Fine granulated sugar termed as 'fine sugar'.

Catfish : (Wolf or Rock fish). It has firm almost boneless, oily flesh, tinged with pink, and is normally available as fillets. Best used for stews and soups. Can be substituted by salmon trout or mackerel.

Catsup : See Ketchup.

Caul : Thin membrane around animals paunch, used for sausage skins.

Cauliflower : A member of the Brassica family, whose creamy-white single fused head of curds is used, and the protective leaves discarded. The variety commonly known as White Cauliflower is, in fact a broccoli, whose head develops into numerous shoots.

Caviar : The salted or marinated hard roe of the sturgeon.

Cayenne Pepper : Dried pods of a red capsicum, which are ground to produce this hot, pungent spice, and should be used sparingly. Do not confuse with chilli powder.

Cecily : See Wild Chervil.

Celeriac : A special variety of celery that is cultivated for its tuberous root. A winter vegetable that is firm to the touch. Can be eaten raw in salads, blanched, steamed, boiled, pureed, or stir-fried.

Celery : The main varieties are the green-ribbed type with large green leaves, and the blanched type with white ribs and yellow leaves. Available all year round, it should have crisp stalks and a good 'heart'. Being crunchy and tangy, it is useful for salads, sandwiches and dips.

Celery Salt : Simply basic salt with additives that give the flavour of salt.

Celery Seeds : Have a slightly bitter taste which goes well with egg and salad-based starters.

Celestine : A garnish made from fine strips of fried pancake, and often used on clear soups.

Cellophane Noodles : (Beanthread Vermicelli) Fine, transparent noodles made from the starch of green mung beans. May be just soaked in hot water, or only very lightly boiled. Can be deep-fried in a dry state when used as a garnish. See transparent noodles.

Celsius : A scale of temperature, where the freezing point of water is 0^0, and the boiling point is 100^0. Also known as Centigrade.

Centigrade : See Celcius.

Cèpe (Fr.) : French name for edible mushrooms.

Cereals : Any grain or edible fruit of the Grass family e.g. wheat, oats, rice, rye, barley, and maize.

Cervelas : A dry or semi-dry variety of large, short sausage of pork and garlic.

Ceylon Moss : See Agar-agar.

Chabot : Freshwater fish with a delicate flavour.

Chad : See Bream.

Chalva : See Halva.

Chamois : Wild venison, best when young, and prepared as roebuck.

Chamomile : A herb used to make herb tea or beer. The oil of this plant is an essential ingredient for flavouring many liqueurs.

Champignon (Fr.) : French for cultivated button mushrooms.

Chanadal (Ind.) : (Channa Dal). A small dark brown variety of chick pea, used mainly in Middle Eastern cooking. See Chick Pea.

Chanterelle : Variety of edible mushroom.

Chantilly (Fr.) : Whipped cream beaten to the consistency of mousse, slightly sweetened and sometimes flavoured with vanilla.

Chap : Lower jaw or half cheek of pig.

Chapati /Chappati /Chuppati (Ind.) : A flat, unleavened Indian bread made from atta whole wheat, millet, maize or chickpea flour.

Chapon : Bread seasoned with garlic, oil and vinegar.

Char : Variety of salmon with delicate flesh resembling trout.

Charcuterie (Fr.) : Cooked products based on pork, such as sausages and terrines.

Chard : See Bream (Sea).

Charentais Melon : A variety of melon fruit which is perfectly round and small, with yellowish-green slightly rough skin marked with downward indentations. The deep orange flesh is faintly scented.

Charlotte : Hot, moulded fruit pudding made of buttered slices of bread and filled with fruit cooked with apricot jam, or a cold moulded dessert consisting of sponge fingers filled with cream and fruit, or, a cream custard set with gelatine.

Charqui : A Chilean dish of dried strips of meat normally Beef, that have been pressed, after salting, then air-dried. They are sautéed, then braised with a mixture of vegetables.

Chartreuse (Fr.) : A French liqueur used in many recipes. Can be green, yellow or white.

Chasselas : Variety of best quality dessert grapes.

Chasse Royal : Roast dish composed of various game joints.

Chasseur (Fr.) : Cooked with mushrooms, shallots and white wine.

Château (Fr.) : Applies to grilled steak or potatoes, cooked in butter.

Chateaubriand : The large steak cut from the centre of a fillet.

Chaud-Froid (Fr.) : Elaborate dish of meat, poultry, game or fish, masked with a creamy sauce, decorated and glazed with aspic. Served cold.

Chawan-Mushi (Jap.) : Steamed foods.

Chayote : (Custard Marrow, Choko, Chow-chow, Vegetable Pear). The pear-shaped fruits, young shoots and roots of this squash are all used and eaten as a vegetable. The young shoots can be boiled and served as asparagus, but it is the fruits that are mainly used, which can be baked or fried, creamed and eaten in desserts and tarts. The flesh can vary from creamy white to a dark green, and unlike many marrows, the flesh remains firm after cooking.

Cheddar Cheese : Probably the most popular of all English cheeses. A strong yellow colour with a close, creamy texture with a full nutty flavour which varies in strength, making it a good all-purpose cheese. Scottish cheddar has a firmer texture, and more often a stronger flavour. Australian and New Zealand cheddar are a deeper yellow with a milder flavour. Canadian cheddar is similar in colour, texture and flavour to English cheddar.

Cheese : A very important form of food for its nutritional value, and is available in a multitude of shapes, sizes and flavours, and has many different uses in the culinary field. It is prepared from the curd precipitated from milk by adding rennin or lactic acid. Cheeses other than cottage or cream varieties, are cured by being left to mature with salt under various types of conditions, that produce the characteristic flavour of that particular type of cheese, such as hard or cream cheese. See also, blue, cottage, processed and whey cheeses. Due to the enormous variety of cheeses available, only the more common names are included alphabetically in this book.

Chemisier : To coat a mould or substance with aspic jelly.

Cherimoya : See Custard Apple.

Cherry : A tasty fruit of which both sweet and acid types are available. Dessert varieties are normally whitish-pink or black, and have a juicy flesh which varies from white-yellow to dark red. The most common acid cherry, is the Morello Cherry which has a dark red skin, and is ideal for making jam or pie ingredient.

Cherry-Bay : (Cherry Laurel). The leaves of this laurel bush produce a bitter almond flavour and smell used in the preparation of various creams. Use very sparingly.

Cherry Plum : A variety of plum.

Chervil : A delicate spicy-flavoured plant similar in appearance to parsley. Should be used fresh either chopped or in sprigs, as a garnish to soups, with delicate fish and shellfish dishes, added to salads and herb butters. The flavour can be destroyed by overcooking. See Bulbous Chervil and Wild Chervil.

Chervis (Chin.) : Plant with a very sweet, aromatic root used for flavouring.

Cheshire Cheese : A British cheese which has a savoury, mellow and slightly salty taste. White Cheshire is really pale yellow in colour. Red Cheshire is coloured with a vegetable dye which makes it look more like red Leicester. It is an excellent cheese for grilling.

Chestnuts : Cannot normally be eaten raw, and must be either boiled, steamed or roasted. They can be purchased fresh, canned or dried, but are much the best when cooked and eaten immediately. Also available as a puree. Can be dried and ground to produce a sweet-flavoured flour used to make Italian porridge. See Polenta and Earthnuts.

Chevrier : A green variety of haricot bean.

Chianti (It.) : Well known, popular Italian red wine.

Chicken : The most common type of poultry which is available under different names according to their age, weight and method of rearing. They are normally available plucked and/or drawn and trussed. Available fresh, frozen, whole or jointed. Fresh chickens should have a plump white breast, smooth and pliable legs, beak and breastbone. A very versatile form of meat which can be used in virtually any method of cooking, but see the different type of chicken suitable for the dish to be prepared, e.g. Pousin, Spring, Roasting, Boiling and Capon.

Chick Peas : (Garbanzo Beans). These large dried peas are usually golden in colour, although there is a small dark brown variety known as Chana Dal used in Middle Eastern dishes. Chick peas have a pleasant crunchy, nutty flavour, and can be used in salads, casseroles, and many savoury dishes. Very popular with vegetarians. A basic ingredient of 'hummus' dips. Available whole or split, they must be soaked well (at least overnight) before long, slow cooking. In a ground form, they produce an excellent flour called gram or besan flour.

Chick Pea Flour : See Gram Flour.

Chicory : (Endive, Belgian Endive, or Witloof). Available all year round, but is best from Autumn to Spring. Should have compact heads with white leaves and yellow-green edges. Can be eaten raw in salads, or braised or boiled either whole or with the stalks separated.

Chicory Gourilos : (Endive stumps). The tender stumps of chicory used as a delicately flavoured vegetable either fried, grilled or braised.

Chiffonade (Fr.) : A garnish made of shredded lettuce, sorrel and spinach. Used for decorating soups or cold dishes.

Chikuwa (Jap.) : Broiled fish cake.

Chillies : The hot flavoured, long, thin, green fruit pods of a variety of the *Capsicum* plant family. Often used fresh either whole or finely chopped as an ingredient in many Eastern and Mediterranean dishes. The seeds of the green variety are the hottest parts, and usually though not always removed. Not to be confused with the large milder *Capsicum Frutescens* or *Annum* varieties. See Red Chillies.

Chillies-Bird's Eye /Bird Peppers : Very small, very hot chillies. Used mainly in pickles, though used in some dishes when a very hot flavour is required. Treat with extreme caution.

Chilling : Cooling food without freezing it, in the refrigerator.

Chilli Oil : A red transparent liquid, bought in small bottles. Very hot, and must be used sparingly.Can be substituted by chilli sauce or tabasco sauce.

Chilli Powder : Produced from red chilli pods, which are dried, and made into flakes or powdered. Popular in both Indian and Mexican dishes. The Mexican variety sometimes contains ground cummin.

Chilli Sauce : A hot red sauce made from red chilli pods, tomatoes, spices, garlic, sugar, vinegar and salt. Similar to tabasco sauce, and normally purchased in a bottle.

Chinchard : See Saurel.

Chine : a pair of loin bones left undivided, from either lamb, mutton, veal, pork or rob of beef.

Chinese Artichoke : Similar to the Jerusalem Artichoke, but it is very small, convoluted and indented, making it tedious to prepare. It has a delicate pleasant flavour with very white flesh.

Chinese Cabbage : (Chinese Mustard, Mustard Greens, Nappa, Pak-choy, Pe-Tsai). A vegetable with long, smooth, tightly-closed leaves with white stems, which resembles a cross between celery and cos lettuce. It has a delicate flavour and a crunchy texture. It can be cooked with meat, poultry or seafoods, and used in soups stir-fries and pickles, or used raw in salads. Can also be used as a wrapping around fillings.

Chinese Cinnamon : See Cinnamon.

Chinese Gooseberry : See Kiwi Fruit.

Chinese Grass : See Agar-agar.

Chinese Mushrooms : They are normally dried, brownish-black in colour, and require soaking for 15-30 minutes before use. They are much stronger and distinctive in taste than fresh mushrooms, and are used sparingly to enhance soups and sauces.

Chinese Parsley : See Coriander.

Chinese Pea : See Mangetout.

Chinese Sausage : A dried sausage, which is sweet and salty. Can be steamed or quick-fried, and normally served with other foods or dishes. Can be substituted by Italian Salami.

Chinese Water Chestnut : A tuber of a sedge, which is normally diced or sliced and used mixed with other vegetables in many Chinese and Oriental dishes. Available fresh or canned.

Chining : Separating the backbone from the ribs in a joint of meat to make carving easier.

Chinois (Fr.) : Prepared in the Chinese style, or a connical-shaped sieve with a fine mesh.

Chipolatas : Very small sausages with skins made of sheep's intestines, from the Italian word for 'Little Fingers'.

Chitterlings : The small intestines of pigs, calves or ox. Can be served cold or fried in a little hot fat.

Chives : A member of the *Liliaceae* onion family, it is a small bushy herb whose hollow stems and bulbs are similar in looks and flavour to onions, but with a much milder flavour. Used mainly as a garnish, chopped, for salads and soups. Does not take kindly to long cooking, and should be added to hot dishes at the last moment. High in vitamins C and B

Chlorophyl : The green colouring matter of all plant materials, which aids plants to produce foodstuffs, with energy derived from sunlight.

Chocolate : A favourite confectionary which is made from cocoa nibs, by refining and adding sugar, cocoa butter, flavourings and lecithin, known as bitter or plain chocolate. Milk solids may be added, which produces milk chocolate.

Choesels (Belg.) : A popular râgout of tripe and beef pancreas.

Choko : See Chayote.

Cholesterol : A form of fat naturally present in animal tissue, produced mainly by the liver.

Cholla : Loaf of white bread made in a twist form, from one thick and one thin piece of dough being plaited together.

Chopping : Cutting all foods into small edible pieces.

Chorizo (Sp.) : Smoked pork and pimiento sausage.

Choux Pastry : Light airy pastry as used in eclairs and profiteroles. The batter is pre-cooked in a saucepan, then piped into round mounds before baking.

Chowchow : See Chayote.

Chowder (U.S.) : Fish dish, half-way between a soup and a stew, often made with clams or shrimps.

Chrine : A savoury Jewish dish of raw beetroot, grated horse-radish, salt, sugar and white vinegar. Makes a good side dish for cold meats and baked potatoes.

Christophene : See Chayote.

Chub : A rather tasteless bony fresh water fish of the carp family.

Chufant : See Tiger Nut.

Chutney : General culinary term for many varied savoury preserves used as condiments.

Chymase /Chymosin : The preferred name for rennet.

Ciabatta (It.) : Bread made with olive oil. Can contain olives, sun-dried tomatoes or walnuts.

Cibol : See Welsh onion.

Cider /Cyder : A beverage made from fermented apple juice. Also an American name for fresh apple juice.

Cieddu (It.) : A form of fermented milk.

Cilantro : See Coriander.

Cinnamon : The dried aromatic bark of an evergreen laurel tree native to Sri Lanka. Best bought in stick, or quill form as the ground spice loses its flavour very quickly when stored too long. It is used in both sweet and savoury dishes. *Cassia,* also known as Chinese Cinnamon, which is grown in India is similar, but much stronger in flavour, and although cheaper, it lacks the delicacy of true cinnamon, particularly in sweet dishes.

Citric Acid : A mild organic acid made from citrus fruit, used for flavouring and preservation purposes.

Citron : The first citrus fruit to be introduced into Europe. It has a very thick peel, solid, sweet, acid-free pulp with virtually no juice. Used extensively for making candied peel.

Citronella : Variety of mint with a very strong aroma.

Citrus Fruit : A genus which includes lemon, orange, grapefruit, tangerine, citron etc.

Civet (Fr.) : Brown game stew or râgout, which includes the essential ingredient of the animals blood.

Clam (U.S.) : An American bi-valve mollusc normally sold live in its shell, but available shelled or canned. Can be served raw like oyster but may be cooked and served as mussels. See Clovisse and Pantella Praire.

Clam Chowder : Popular soup of clams and salted pork.

Claret : English name for red Bordeaux wine.

Clarification : A culinary term for clearing fats and suspended particles by heating and filtering, or adding flocculating agents such as isinglass. Also clearing consommés and jellies with beaten egg white.

Clarified Butter : (Ghee). Butter cleared of water and impurities by slowly melting and filtering, allowing for use in cooking with higher temperatures.

Clary : Variety of sage herb used in pastry.

Clear Soup : A consommé to which has been added various garnishes to flavour and enhance the liquid stock.

Clementine : A cross between an orange and a tangerine with a stiff orange-like skin. It is virtually seedless, and the pink-tinged flesh is slightly acidic, but has a refreshing taste without being too sweet.

Clod : The meat joint from the upper part of a bullock's shoulder. Suitable for stewing, braising or pies and puddings.

Clotted Cream : Double cream that is scolded to reduce liquid content, and thus solidify.

Clotting : Applying a gentle heat to cream in order to thicken.

Cloud : A term applied to liquid that for some reason is no longer clear.

Cloves : The dried flower buds of an evergreen tropical tree native to Southeast Asia. Can be bought ground, but are best whole to retain their very strong sweet, pungent and aromatic flavour, and should therefore be used sparingly. Oil of cloves contains phenol, a powerful antiseptic that discourages putrefaction, and is hence used to preserve food.

Clovisse : Variety of clam that can be either eaten raw like oysters, or cooked as mussels.

Clupeidae : A family of fish which includes herring, sardine and anchovy.

Coagulate : To thicken or congeal, particularly with regards to fat.

Coalfish : See Coley.

Cob : The centre of a large ear of grain to which the grains are attached. Most commonly associated with 'corn on the cob', which is cooked whole and the corn or maize is eaten from the cob.

Cobnut : See Hazelnut.

Cochineal : (Carmine). A red colouring agent, made from the female *Conchilla* Cacti.

Cock : Common culinary term for chicken.

Cock-A-Leekie : Scottish soup made from chicken and leeks.

Cockle : (Venus). A small bi-valve mollusc, which can be eaten raw with vinegar and pepper, or boiled for about 6 minutes, and added to various sea-food platters and dishes, or used as an addition to fish soups and sauces.

Cocoa /Cacao /Kakayo : The name is derived from the seeds embedded in the fruit of the *Cacao* plant.

Cocoa Nibs : The seeds of the *Cacao* plant fruit that have been left to ferment, which modifies the bitterness and darkens the colour. They are then roasted and separated from the husks as two halves of the seed, and thus known as nibs. Used to make chocolate and cocoa beverages and confectionaries.

Cocolait : A form of coconut milk, made by pressing the coconut under high pressure and then homogenising.

Coconut : A delectable sweet 'fleshy' nut, especially useful in Indonesian and West Indian dishes. But is also very popular in sweets, cakes and puddings. Available fresh or dried and flaked. The milk is extracted and the flesh may be pounded into a cream, or processed and desiccated or shredded. It is very high in saturated fats. The dried nut is known as Copra.

Coconut Milk : This is not the 'water' found inside the nut, as is commonly believed, but the creamy liquid extracted from the grated flesh of fresh coconuts or from desiccated (shredded) coconut. The flavour of this milk has no substitute.

Coco Plum : A tropical fruit eaten raw, or is dried like plums.

Cocose : Butter made from coconut oil.

Cocotte (Fr.) : Small ovenproof, earthenware, porcelain or metal dish, used for baking individual egg dishes, mousses or souffles.

Cod : A very large, highly nutritious fish with firm white flesh, which is suitable for all methods of cooking.

Cod-Burbot : See Burbot.

Coddle : To very lightly boil an egg until it has only just set.

Coddling : Cooking slowly (normally eggs), by steaming over simmering water, just below boiling point.

Cod Liver Oil : An oil made from cods livers. Seldom used in cooking, but is high in vitamins A and D.

Cod Roe : Smoked roe is an excellent substitute for grey mullet roe in making taramasalata. It should be soaked in fresh water to remove the strong salty taste, when it is then perfect for grilling, and eaten as a snack on toast with tomato sauce.

Coffee : A favourite beverage which comes in many different blends, but it is all produced from the berries of either the *Arabica* or *Robusta Coffea* shrub. It contains caffeine, an alkaloid drug, which raises blood pressure, stimulates the kidneys, and temporarily averts fatigue. This however, can be removed and is then known as 'Decaffeinated Coffee', but some of the natural flavour and aroma is lost during the process.

Coffee Essence : An aqueous extract of roasted coffee, used to either make a beverage, or as a flavouring.

Cola : An extract of cola beans, normally associated with carbonated drinks. Contains caffeine. Can also be added to various cream dishes and cakes.

Colander : Perforated metal or plastic bowl used for draining away liquids.

Colbert : A term used to describe fish that are egg-and-crumb coated before frying.

Cole : A type of rape kale. See Rape.

Coleslaw : A variety of salad made from finely shredded raw cabbage heart, carrot, onion, vinegar and seasonings.

Coley : (Saithe, Rock Salmon or Coalfish) It has a near black skin with a dark pinkish-grey flesh which turns white when cooked. Always sold in fillets, and is suitable for grilling, baking or frying. Can be used in place of cod or haddock.

Colin : See Hake.

Collage : A term that describes the clarification of alcoholic beverages.

Collared Beef : A flank of beef that is first marinaded, then boned, rolled and tied, and very slowly boiled or casseroled.

Collards : Variety of spring greens.

Colle : See Gelatine.

Collops : A very rich, savoury form of Shepherds pie.

Colocasi /Cologasi : A rare tuberous vegetable, grown mainly in Cyprus. Can be used as a potato substitute.

Colonne : Utensil used to core apples or slice vegetables into thick lengths.

Comfits : Fruit or vegetables preserved in either sugar, vinegar or brandy.

Compote (Fr.) : Dessert of fresh or dried fruit, cooked in syrup and served cold. Also a stew made from small birds or fowl.

Comte Cheese (Fr.) : A firm yellowish cheese, which is good for cooking.

Concasse (Fr.) : Roughly chopped. Applied to vegetables such as tomatoes.

Conde (Fr.) : Desserts always made with rice, e.g. pear conde.

Condiment : Seasoning normally added at the table after serving food to improve its flavour, such as salt, pepper, mustard and ginger.

Conditioning : A term normally referring to meat that is being hung to allow the natural production of Lactic acid, which gradually improves the texture and keeping qualities of the meat. For flour and wine, see Ageing.

Coney : See Burbot.

Confectionary : A term used to describe the culinary production of sweets.

Confectioners Glucose : See Glucose Syrup.

Confit : Any meat that is cooked and then preserved in its' own fat or juices.

Confiture : Any fruit jams, pastes and sweetmeats, or fruit stewed in thick syrup.

Congee : A rice pudding or porridge.

Conger Eel : (Garfish). The most common sea-eel. A strongly flavoured eel with firm hard flesh, used mainly in pies, and braises well. Can be smoked, and served cold. Can be substituted with lamprey.

Conserve : Whole fruit preserved by boiling in sugar and used like jam.

Consommé (Fr.) : Meat stock or bouillon that has been enriched, concentrated and clarified. Also a name for a clear soup.

Cookie (U.S.) : American term for biscuit.

Cooking : A process to make food more palatable and digestible, by breaking down the connective tissue in meat and softening the cellulose in plant tissues. There are many different methods used to achieve this result, depending on the food in question, and ones personal preference, the main types of cooking being:-

a) Boiling - cooking in a liquid at boiling point or above.

b) Braising - browning in hot fat then stewing.

c) Broiling /Grilling - heating over or under a direct flame.

d) Deep-frying - Completely immersing the food in hot fat or oil.

e) Devilled - grilled or fried after coating a marinade, herbs or breadcrumbs.

f) Fricassee - a combination of saute and stewing.

g) Frying - cooking in hot fat or oil on a hob.

h) Pan-broiling - cooking on hot, dry metal over direct heat.

i) Poaching - gently simmering in a liquid.

j) Pot-roasting - slow method of steaming.

k) Pressure cooking - a fast method of steaming.

l) Roasting - cooking with radiant heat.

m) Sautéeing - Frying in a pan with a small amount of fat or liquid.

n) Simmering - cooking in water which is just below boiling point.

o) Spit-roasting - rotating skewered food over an open fire or heat.

p) Steaming - cooking by heat conveyed by steam either directly or through a jacket.

q) Stewing - prolonged simmering.

Coot : Similar to moorhen with dark, dry flesh and medium flavoured. Can be cooked as duck.

Copra : Dried coconut meat used for making oil, margarine or soap.

Coq (Fr.) : French word for cock.

Coqueret : See Strawberry Tomato.

Coquille (Fr.) : A scallop shellfish, or a shell-shaped ovenproof dish used to serve fish or poultry delicacies.

Coral Roe : Orange roe of shellfish or lobster. Cook as hard roe.

Corder : A term used to describe pastry to which too much water has been added during the mixing, causing very hard results.

Coriander Fresh : (Chinese Parsley, Cilantro, Dhaniya). Often confused with certain types of parsley, the coriander leaves have an orangy pungent flavour, and are an indispensable ingredient of curries especially in conjunction with green chillies, garlic and green ginger. Can be substituted with parsley.

Coriander Seed : Available whole or ground, and is one of the main ingredients in curry powder, and although not hot, its mild, slightly bitter taste and fragrance would definitely be missed if not included. The seeds can be roasted to bring out a more curry-like flavour.

Corm : The thickened underground base of plant stems, often known as bulbs, e.g. onions.

Corn : (Maize). An extremely versatile grain that yields many useful products. Available as whole or cracked grains, it comes in many varieties and has several by-products, such as popcorn, sweetcorn, dentcorn, cornmeal and cornflour.

Corn Bread : (Pone Bread). A loaf which uses dough made from corn grits.

Corned Beef : Diced beef which has been cured in salt and sugar, then pressed and canned.

Cornel : See Cornelian Cherry.

Cornelian Cherry : (Cornel). A very tart variety of cherry mainly used to make jelly.

Cornet : A term used to describe thin pieces of meat or pastry rolled to form a cone.

Corn Flakes : Breakfast cereal made from flaked grains of maize.

Cornflour : (Cornstarch). Finely ground purified starch prepared from maize, used to thicken soups, sauces, custard and blancmange etc. Can be used to substitute arrowroot.

Corngrits : Flour made from grinding hominy.

Cornish Cream : The same as Devonshire cream, but the original cream is scolded without the skimmed milk.

Cornmeal : When ground to a powder, this corn grain can be made into porridge, or used in cakes, desserts and pancakes.

Corn Oil : A very light oil with hardly any flavour, which makes it perfect for stir-fries, deep-frying and salad dressings.

Corn Salad : (Lambs Lettuce, Dragonet). Similar to normal lettuce, but with long thin leaves and very little flavour. The only advantage of this plant over lettuce, is that the leaves can be picked outside during the winter. Can also be cooked as spinach.

Corn Starch (U.S.) : See Cornflour.

Corn Syrup (U.S.) : See Glucose Syrup.

Cos Lettuce : (Romaine). Variety of salad lettuce with firm, crisp, oblong green leaves and a pale green heart, and a sweetish taste, that keep well. See Round Lettuce and Iceberg.

Cote : A rib slice of beef or veal.

Cotelettes : Small cutlets or slices of meat, normally from the best end of neck.

Cotignac : Paste made from quince.

Cotriade : Fish dish similar to bouillabaisse, using mainly oily fish.

Cottage Cheese : Soft uncured white cheese made from pasteurised skimmed milk or milk powder, and a lactic acid starter with or without rennet, which is then heated, washed and drained. It is low in calories, almost pure white, with a very bland flavour.

Cotton Seed : For culinary purposes, it is mainly used as a valuable source of cooking oil.

Coucher : A term used to describe the operation of piping a mixture with a forcing bag to form either a round or oblong shape.

Coulibiac (Russ.) : Hot fish pie made from either salmon or sterlet.

Coulis : Essentially a thick sauce. Meat juices which are produced during cooking, a thick soup made from crustaceans or a thick fruit syrup.

Coulommiers Cheese (Fr.) : A soft, yellowish cream cheese, which has a white crust tinged with grey. It has a stronger, less mellow taste than brie, and has a faint almond flavour.

Coupe (Fr.) : Goblet used for serving ice cream, fruit and shellfish cocktails.

Courgette : (Zucchini, Baby, Italian Marrows). A member of the gourd family. A compact bush fruit, which is grown exclusively to produce this immature fruit. The most popular variety is zucchini, which can be eaten raw in salads, or cooked separately as a hot vegetable, or as an ingredient in many vegetable/savoury dishes.

Court Boullion : Seasoned aromatic liquid in which meat, poultry, fish or vegetables are either boiled or poached.

Couscous : Processed semolina which is formed into very small pellets. Also a national dish from North Africa and Asia dish made from couscous, mutton or chicken and merga.

Cousinette : Soup made from only green vegetable leaves and green herbs.

Cover : To add just enough water or stock to submerge all of the food to be cooked.

Cow : In culinary terms. The meat of sterile cows or heifers.

Cow's Heel : The foot of a cow used to make a jellied stock. See Neats' Foot.

Cow's Milk : A complete protein food which is particularly rich in protein. Tastes its best when 'unprocessed', but is available 'skimmed' which has all the goodness but only 1% of the original fat content, which however results in a 'watery' flavour and consistency. Available dried which can be useful baking, or adding to soups or drinks.

Crab : A crustacean which is grey-brown when alive, and brownish-red when cooked. It is sometimes sold alive, but is usually freshly boiled by the fishmonger. Can also be purchased 'dressed' i.e. cooked and prepared ready for eating. The claws contain the white meat, and the shell the brown meat.

Crab Apple : A small, very sharp tasting apple variety, used mainly for making jams and jellies.

Crack : The degree of cooking sugar towards its caramelisation. See Caramel.

Cracked Wheat : See Bulgur.

Crackling : The crisp skin taken from a joint of roasted pork, usually cut into thin slices, and eaten either with the main dish or as a savoury side-dish.

Cracknel : A dry petit-four biscuit.

Cramique (Bel) : Variety of Brioche bread made with raisins.

Cranberry : (Mossberry). Small American fruit similar to bilberry. The skins are lustrous, and varying in colour from pink to dark red. They have a sharp, slightly bitter taste and are used mainly for making preserves and sauces. Used as a condiment with game and fowl dishes.

Craquelin : A very dry, crunchy type of cake.

Crawfish (U.S.) : See Crayfish.

Crayfish : (Crawfish, Rocklobster or Spiny Lobster). A freshwater crustacean similar to a lobster, but heavier, weighing about 5-7 lbs. It is red even before cooking, but has no main large claws, and all the meat is contained in the 'tail'. The flesh is firmer in texture than lobster meat, and more delicately flavoured, but is prepared in the same way. The 'tails' can be purchased frozen. See Lobster.

Cream : The fatty part of milk, of which there are various types, depending mainly on the percentage of fat content. Single cream is normally less than 18% fat content, Double or Thick cream should be 48% fat, Clotted cream should be not less than 48%, and Whipping cream not less than 35%. See individual headings for descriptions and uses, including Cornish, Devonshire and Synthetic.

Cream Cheese : Cheese made from whole milk, enriched with extra cream to which rennet has been added during the process.

Creaming : Working together a mixture such as fat and sugar with a wooden spoon, until light and fluffy, liked whipped cream.

Cream Of Tartar : (Tartaric Acid). A raising agent in self-raising flour, or mixed with bicarbonate of soda to produce baking powder.

Creams : A general term applied to a whole variety of butter, whipped cream and custard creams. Used to make sauces, soups and pastry garnishes.

Crécy : A term applied to preparations garnished or dominated by carrots.

Crème (Fr.) : French term for fresh cream, butter, custard creams, and thick creamy soups.

Crème a La : Dishes whose pan juices have been added to fresh cream to produce the sauce.

Crème Anglaise : Custard.

Crème Brulee (Fr.) : Cream custard with caramelised topping.

Crème Caramel (Fr.) : Cold moulded egg custard with caramel topping.

Crème de Gruyere (Fr.) : Processed Gruyere cheese, which is soft and mild, and normally sold in portions.

Crème Fraiche (Fr.) : Cream that has been allowed to mature but not to go sour.

Créole : Of Caribbean cookery; prepared with pimentos, tomatoes, okra, rice and spicy sauces.

Crêpe (Fr.) : Thin pancake of eggs and flour.

Crêpes Suzette (Fr.) : Pancakes cooked in orange sauce and flamed in a liqueur.

Crépinette : Small, flat sausage made from meat covered with a layer of forcemeat.

Cress : See Watercress.

Crimping : Making a decorative border to pie crusts. Gashing fresh skate, then soaking it in cold water and vinegar before cooking, so that the flesh firms. Also a term for removing v-cuts from salad vegetables, such as cucumbers, radishes and carrots using a canelle knife to produce a decorative effect.

Crispbread : A hard, dry wafer made from wheat or rye flour and very little water, and therefore much drier than 'normal' Bread.

Croissant : Crescent-shaped roll made from puff pastry or leavened dough.

Crop : The pouch of the gullet in grain-eating game or poultry birds.

Croquets : Small dry almond-flavoured biscuits

Croquettes (Fr.) : Cooked foods moulded in small shapes, dipped in egg and crumbs, and deep-fried. Refers to both meat, vegetable or sweet preparations.

Croustade (Fr.) : Small crispy fried or baked bread or pastry shape which is filled with a savoury mixture.

Croûtes (Fr.) : Pastry covering meat, fish and vegetables. Or, slices of bread or brioche, spread with butter or sauce, and baked until crisp, used as a base for serving savoury mixtures, or as a garnish.

Croûtons (Fr.) : Small cubes of de-crusted bread fried briskly in hot butter or oil and used to garnish soups and dishes served with a sauce. Crushed garlic can be added to the oil before heating. See Sippets.

Crowdie Cheese : A Scottish type of cottage cheese made from skimmed milk. The grains are finer than those of ordinary cottage cheese and has a mild, fresh flavour. High in protein.

Crown : A term used to describe dishes that are presented in the shape of a crown or ring.

Crown Roast : A loin of lamb chops, cut from the bone enough to allow the joint to be rolled and formed into a circle, and then roasted.

Cruet : Dispensers for the table which contain seasonings, generally salt, pepper and mustard.

Crumble : To break into very small pieces or crumbs, by rubbing between the thumb and fingers.

Crumpets : Dough cakes which have had sodium bicarbonate added to the batter.

Crust : The outer part of a loaf, or the pastry covering of pies and puddings.

Crustaceans : A group of shellfish such as crabs, crayfish, lobsters and shrimps, which have jointed shells. See Molluscs.

Crystal Rice : (Cristallo, Italian rice, Riso). A variety of short oval-grained rice, which absorbs a large amount of liquid during cooking, and produces a moist, sticky mass. Used mainly for desserts rather than savoury dishes, although used extensively in Italian cooking

Cube : To cut or dice food into reasonably small squares.

Cucumber : A common vegetable of the *Cucumis Sativus*, which is a member of the gourd family. It has a refreshing crisp flavour, and is used extensively in salads, sliced and eaten raw, but can be used in soups, or as a garnish.

Cucurbits : A gourd produced from the *Cucurbitaceae* plant. See Gourds.

Culinary Methods : See Cooking.

Cumin : (Cummin, Jeera). Available as whole small, half crescent-shaped seeds, or ground like coriander, and is an essential ingredient in curry powders. Being hot and pungent, with a nutty aroma, it must not be confused with caraway seed, which is very similar in appearance, and both are used in breads and cakes.

Cummin Black : This is not true cummin, and the flavour quite different, being aromatic and peppery.

Cummin Sweet : See Fennel.

Curaçao : A liqueur made from the rind of Seville oranges and brandy or gin. Can be used for flavouring desserts, creams and sauces.

Curcuma : A yellow rhizome with a bitter flavour similar to saffron, which, when ground, is used to flavour curries. See Saffron.

Curd : Semi-solid part of fresh milk or clotted protein, which has been treated with rennet, and is the basic ingredient of cheese. The fluid remaining after the process is known as whey.

Curdle : To cause fresh milk or sauce to separate into solids and liquids by heating and adding acid or rennet, or to cause creamed butter and sugar in a cake recipe to separate by adding the eggs too rapidly. It is also the first stage in cheese making.

Cure : To preserve fish or meat by drying, salting or smoking.

Curing : A pickling process which permits the growth of only salt-tolerant bacteria. Normally used for meat, which preserves and prevents harmful bacteria growth.

Currants : Fruit of the *Ribes.* Either white, red or a translucent black. See Dried Currants.

Curry : A term used to describe mainly Eastern dishes, where the combined mixtures of many spices are fried to release their flavours and aromas before adding the main ingredients of the dish.

Curry Beans : See Lima Beans.

Curry Leaves : The aromatic leaves of the *Sweet Nim* tree native to Asia. They are small and very shiny. Although difficult to find fresh, they do retain their unique 'curry' smell when dried. As important to curries as bayleaves are to stews, especially in vegetable dishes, where they release an appetising smell whilst cooking.

Curry Powder : A mixture of various ground spices which can be used for making curries. Although a convenient commodity, there is no substitute for grinding and roasting the individual spices, as most spices do not retain their flavour for a long period after being ground.

Cushaw : Variety of marrow or squash family.

Custard : A dessert made from milk mixed with either custard powder, or eggs, sweetener and flavourings.

Custard Apple : (Bullock's Heart). Name given to the *Anona sop* family group of very large tropical fruits, with tender green skins, white flesh and an abundance of black seeds. Includes sweet or sour sop and cherimoya.

Custard Cream : A basic custard mixture of egg yolks, castor sugar and boiling milk, flavoured with vanilla and lemon or orange zest.

Custard Marrow : See Chayote.

Custard Powder : Usually maize starch, which has been coloured and flavoured.

Cuttle Fish : A mollusc with an internal shell, with tough flesh. Cook as Octopus. See also squid.

Dab : A flat fish, which can be used either whole or filleted, and could be used in place of brill or plaice as a cheap substitute.

Dace : (Dard). A freshwater fish with tough flesh, normally used in a fish stew or matelote.

Dadhi (Ind.) : A form of fermented milk.

Dahlia : Ornamental plant whose tubers are cooked as, and have the flavour of Jerusalem artichokes.

Daikon (Jap.) : A large white Japanese radish, resembling a parsnip. Can be substituted by small sweet turnips. See Radish.

Daizu (Jap.) : See Soybean.

Dahl : A mixture of lentils, butter and curry powder, and cooked to produce a thick soup.

Dal : The Indian name for pulses.

Damascenes : Small Damson plums.

Dampfrudeln (Ger.) : A popular German pastry.

Damson : A small dark-skinned variety of plum, used mainly for jam making.

Danablu : See Danish Blue Cheese.

Danbo Cheese : A mild-flavoured and firm textured Danish cheese, which is easily recognisable by its regular, even-sized holes. It has a thick almost inedible crust.

Danish Blue Cheese : A white cheese with a strong salty flavour, which, with its close blue veins, diminishes with maturity. Made from homogenised milk with a high cream content, it has a soft, slightly creamy texture.

Dariole : Small cup-shaped mould used for making puddings, sweet and savoury jellies, and creams.

Darne (Fr.) : Thick cut or slice of a round fish.

Dartois : Small pieces of light crisp pastry, baked and used as a base for hors-d'oeuvres, or as a garnish.

Dash : A general small measure to mean a 'pinch' or 'splash' of an ingredient.

Dasheen : See Eddoe.

Dashi (Jap.) : Stock made from kambu seaweed and fried bonito fish. Used in many Japanese recipes. Available in sachets or dried granules.

Date : Fresh dates are plump, shiny fruits and yellow-red to golden brown in colour with smooth skins, with a sugary-sweet pulpy flesh. Dried dates should still be plump and shiny, with no sugary crystals.

Date Plum : See Permission.

Daube (Fr.) : Stew of meat, normally beef, and vegetables cooked in stock.

Daun Pandan : See Pandanus.

Daun Salam (Ind.) : An aromatic leaf used mainly in Indonesian cooking. It is larger than a curry leaf, but has a similar flavour, and makes a good substitute.

Daurade : See Bream.

Decant : To pour liquid from one container to another. Normally applies to wine which is carefully poured into decanters to separate from the sediment before serving.

Decoction : Boiling a solid food, generally meat, for a long period to produce a stock or clear soup.

Deep Fat : Hot fat which is deep enough to totally immerse food during frying.

Deep-Frying : Frying food by completely immersing it in hot fat or oil. The food is normally egg-and-crumbed or coated in batter before frying. Drain well after cooking to remove excess fat.

Deer : **(Roebuck)**. A mammal whose distinctive flesh is known as Venison.

Déglacer (Fr.) : Diluting pan juices by adding wine, stock or cream to make gravy.

Dégorger : To draw out moisture, e.g. salting aubergines to remove bitter juices, or to soak food in cold water to remove impurities or unwanted flavours.

Dehydrate : A method of preserving foodstuffs such as fruit, eggs, vegetables, by removing all traces of water. Before using, these items must be reconstituted by soaking in water.

Demerara Sugar : Light brown crystals of sucrose produced during the process of making fully refined white crystals or table sugar.

Demersal Fish : Those living near the bottom of the sea, and contain little oil, e.g. cod, haddock, or halibut. See also Pelagic Fish.

Demi-Glace : A versatile sauce or half-glaze made from reduced meat juices, or espagnole and white stock. Often enhanced with sherry for flavour.

Demi-Sol Cheese (Fr.) : A small, square, fresh cream cheese, with very little salt and tasting almost like cream. Normally sold in small wrapped portions.

Dent Corn : A fairly hard variety of maize, which is normally ground into meal or flour.

Derby Cheese : A honey-coloured, close-textured cheese which has to mature for at least 6 months to develop its mild, distinctive flavour.

Desiccation : A method of preserving solid foodstuffs by drying or dehydrating.

Dessert : (Sweet). Normally the last course of a meal, which can include cheese, sweets or fruit.

Devil Fish : See Angler.

Devilling : Preparing meat, poultry or fish by slitting open, then spreading flat and seasoning well, before grilling or roasting.

Devil's Tongue (Jap.) : A Japanese vegetable.

Devonshire Cream : A variety of clotted cream, that is made by floating a layer of double cream on to skimmed milk, scolded and then skimmed off. The resultant thick clotted cream should be about 63% fat.

Dewberry : A large variety of blackberry, but with a different flavour.

Dextrins : A mixture of soluble compounds formed by a partial breakdown of starch by heat, acid or enzymes. Formed when bread is toasted. Complete breakdown yields maltose.

Dextrose : Pure Glucose or grape sugar.

Dhal (Ind.) : An Indian term for Split Peas or Lentils.

Dhaniya : See Coriander.

Diablotins : Small poached gnocchi, spiced with cayenne pepper, sprinkled with grated cheese, then lightly grilled just before serving.

Dicing : Cutting food into small cubes.

Diet : A general term used to describe the combination of foods that need to be eaten in order to survive in a healthy state.

Dietary Fibre : The natural fibre found in grain products, that is an essential part of our daily diet, in order to assist the excretory process.

Digestive Biscuits : Crisp wheatmeal biscuits, often eaten with cheese.

Dijon Mustard (Fr.) : A French mustard that is very useful in cooking as it is fairly 'pure', as unlike most other mustards, it contains no tarragon, sugar or vinegar.

Dill : A herb of the parsley family, of which both the leaves and seeds may be used, the seeds having a slightly sharper, more bitter taste than the leaves, which may be used either fresh or dried. Used to make pickles, flavour sauces, salad dressings and mayonnaise, or as a garnish to fish soups, and to flavour lamb and mutton stews. It has a distinctive flavour, which can be lost during cooking and should only be added at the last minute. Can be a substitute for fennel.

Diluting : To add one liquid to another to reduce its solidity.

Dipper : A large ladle used to remove stocks or soups from their cooking vessels.

Disjoint : To cut an animal or fowl into sections at each joint.

Dissolve : To add a liquid to dry ingredients until they melt.

Distil : To separate alcohol from a liquid by vaporisation.

Ditali : The largest size tubes of cut macaroni.

Doe : Female deer whose meat (venison), is inferior to buck (male deer).

Dogfish : See Huss.

Dolcelatte (It.) : A famous Italian veined cheese. It is off-white with blue-green veins running through it, with a full, robust flavour and a moist creamy texture.

Dolic : A group of pulses that includes soybean.

Dolmas : A popular Turkish dish of vine leaves stuffed with rice and minced lamb. Can also apply to various stuffed vegetables, such as aubergines or courgettes.

Dorade : See Bream.

Dorure : Beaten egg yolks used for brushing pastry etc.

Dosas (Ind.) : A pancake made from ground rice, pulses or lentils. Can be eaten plain or with a savoury filling.

Dot : To scatter or strew small pieces of butter, cheese or other diced ingredients over the top of a food preparation.

Double consommé : Consommé which has either been reduced by half, or strengthened by bouillon cubes.

Double Gloucester : A famous golden-coloured mature cheese with a crumbly texture, and a distinct 'bite', but should never be pungent. See also Single Gloucester.

Double Pousin : A young chicken 6 to 10 weeks old, weighing about 2 lbs. Cook as Pousin, but serves two.

Double Saucepan /Boiler : A two-part saucepan with a top pan fitted into a lower one that holds simmering water. Used for slow, gentle cooking of food that must not come into contact with direct heat.

Double /Thick Cream : A thick cream that should have 48% fat content.

Dough : Various mixtures of flour, water, milk, and /or egg, sometimes enriched with fat, with or without yeast, kneaded, rolled and shaped.

Dough Cakes : Snack foods such as crumpets, muffins and pikelets, which are made from a batter mixture of flour, water and milk, raised with yeast, and baked on a hot-plate.

Doughnuts : An individual round light dough cake, which has been fried in deep fat. Often filled with jam and /or cream.

Dover Sole : See Sole (Dover).

Doyenne : Very sweet soft-fleshed dessert pear.

Dragonet : See Corn Salad.

Dragon's Eyes: (Loong Ngaan) Similar to small lychees, with succulent flesh and a round pip in the middle. Normally sold canned.

Drain : To strain food from any liquid in which it has been cooked, or to place fried or grilled food on absorbent cloth to remove excess oil or fat before serving.

Drambuie : A whisky based liqueur, flavoured with herbs and honey.

Draw /Drawn : To remove the entrails from poultry or game, or a bird that has had the entrails removed.

Drawn Butter : Melted butter mixed with flour, nutmeg, water, wine and either salt or sugar, then cooked until thickened, and served with either vegetables or puddings.

Dredge : To sprinkle flour or sugar evenly over food. This is often done prior to frying fish or meat, or after cooking pastries such as cakes, biscuits and pancakes.

Dress : To pluck, draw and truss poultry or game, or to arrange or garnish a cooked dish, or to prepare cooked shellfish in their shells, e.g. crab and lobster.

Dressing : Sauce for a salad, consisting basically of two parts olive oil to one part wine vinegar. Or stuffing for meat and poultry.

Dried Currants : Small seedless black grapes that have been dried out, preferably in the sun.

Dried Gourd Strips : These are mainly used in Chinese and Japanese cooking, where they are reconstituted or cooked in liquid, soups and stews.

Dried Mango : See Amchoor.

Dried Mushrooms : Dehydrated mushrooms, which, when simmered in water or stock, provide an aromatic broth.

Dried Shrimp Paste (Ind.) : Also known as Belacan or Blachan. A pungent paste made from prawns, and used in many Southeast Asian recipes. It is sold in cans or flat slabs, or cakes, and will keep indefinitely if stored in a tightly sealed jar, without refrigeration. Can be substituted by Maldive fish.

Dried Vegetables : The only method of preserving vegetables which still retains all their nutrients. A useful way of storing delicate items such as funghi and seaweed, which can often be hard to obtain.

Dripping : Unbleached and untreated fat obtained from meat or bones of animals or birds while roasting. Used for basting meat and for making meat pie pastry to add flavour.

Dropping Consistency : A test to determine the correct consistency of cake and pudding mixtures prior to cooking, by tilting a spoonful, when the mixture should fall from the spoon within a few seconds.

Drumstick Bean (Ind.) : See Green Bean.

Drupes : Botanical name for fruit that has a single seed, surrounded by a stone, then flesh, such as plums.

Dry Frying : Frying without the use of fat, by either the use of non-stick pans, or vegetable extract.

Dry Ice : Solid carbon dioxide which produces -790° C. Mainly used for transporting cold foods.

Drying : To preserve fruit, vegetables, or herbs by dehydrating.

Dry Shell Bean : American name for dried haricot bean.

Dubarry : Cauliflower served with Mornay sauce.

Dublin Bay Prawns : (Langoustine, Nephrop, Norway Lobster, Scampi). The largest British prawn, about 4 ins. long, and pale pink with a hard shell. Available alive or cooked, with or without shells, it has a delightfully subtle flavour, and ideal in either hot or cold dishes.

Duchesse : A mixture of puréed potato, egg yolks, milk and butter, which is piped into shapes with a forcing bag, then lightly browned.

Duck : A fatty bird normally weighing about 4-6 lbs., but allow more weight per person than for chicken. The breast should be plump, the bird's underbill soft enough to bend, and the feet pliable. Available fresh or frozen. The favourite culinary variety is the white-feathered Aylesbury Duck.

Duckling : A young duck weighing 3-4 lbs. Will only serve two, and is normally roasted.

Dudi : A cucumber-looking member of the Marrow or Squash family, originally from Africa and the West Indies.

Dulse : Reddish-purple edible seaweed. Can be eaten raw or cooked.

Dumpling : Small balls made of dough, forcemeat or potato mixture, which are steamed or poached. Used to garnish soups and stews, or fruit encased in dough and baked.

Dunelin : A dish of braised mutton and vegetables.

Dunlop Cheese : A moist Scottish cheese, rather like English cheddar but with a softer texture and usually milder in flavour with the colour of pale butter. Good for grilling.

Dunst : Very fine semolina.

Durum Wheat : A main type of hard wheat grain grain used to make semolina for pastas and couscous.

Dust : To lightly sprinkle a preparation with flour, fine sugar, spice or seasoning mainly for decoration purposes.

Dutch Cocoa : Cocoa that has been treated with a dilute solution of alkali to improve the colour, flavour and solubility.

Dutch Oven : A semi-circular metal shield with shelves, placed close to an open fire, used for roasting.

Dwarf Bean : See French Bean.

Earthnut : Tuberous black-skinned root with white flesh, which tastes like, and is prepared as chestnuts, and can be used as a substitute.

Eat-All Peas : See Mangetout Beans.

Échaudé : Pastry where the dough is poached in water, then oven-dried.

Echauder : A French term meaning to scald.

Éclair : Light, oblong choux pastry split and filled with cream, and usually topped with chocolate icing.

Ecossaise : Mutton stew with barley and vegetables.

Écuelle : A device for obtaining peel oil from citrus fruit.

Edam Cheese : This Dutch cheese has a mild flavour and a rather rubbery consistency. It is always encased in a red wax rind. Similar in flavour to Gouda cheese, but not as creamy, as Edam is made from partly skimmed milk.

Eddoe : (Dasheen, Kandalla, Satoimo, Taro). A tuber similar in appearance to a thick-skinned potato. It has a nutty flavour, low in water content, and high in starch and protein. Cook as potatoes.

Edelpilz Cheese (Ger) : This German cheese is white around the edges and mottled blue in the centre, with a strong flavour and a crumbly texture.

Edge Bone : See Aitch Bone.

Eel : This common eel is a richly flavoured freshwater fish with a slender body up to three feet long, and has firm white flesh. Normally sold live, as they should be cooked as soon as possible after killing. Steam, braise or deep-fry. Can be purchased smoked, or 'jellied', which is a required taste, but a firm favourite amongst true Londoners, where they are a local delicacy. See Conger Eel for the seawater variety.

Effervescence : The release of gas from a liquid.

Egg : Probably the most important and versatile cooking ingredient, used in a whole range of preparations. Can also be eaten alone, either raw, boiled, poached, scrambled or fried.

Egg-And-Crumb : Coating food with an egg and breadcrumb mixture before baking or frying, which helps to reduce the amount of fat absorbed by the coated food during cooking.

Eggnog : A drink made from egg yolks, milk, flavourings and brandy.

Egg Plant : See Aubergine.

Eggs-Chinese : Also known as 'Ancient' or '1,000 year-old' eggs because they appear to have been buried for decades. In fact they are unshelled pickled eggs, which have been buried in earth, lime and chopped straw for 1-2 months. When shelled, their insides are dark, pungent, and savoury. Can be eaten with soft rice, or as an hors d'oeuvres.

Eggwhite : The outer layer of an egg surrounding the yolk. The 'thin' whites produce more froth and are best for beating, and 'thick' whites are best for frying or poaching as it coagulates.

Egyptian Lentils : See Green Lentils.

Eiweiss Milch : See Protein Milk.

Elderflower : The white fragrant flowers of the *Elder* tree, used to flavour jams and wines.

Elk : See Moose.

Elvers : Minute, transparent, freshly spawned eels, which are boiled to form a jelly, and eaten on bread, or as a side dish with salad.

Embden Groats : Groats that have been crushed.

Emblic : (Indian Gooseberry). A berry of the *Malacca* tree resembling a gooseberry. Rich in vitamin C.

Embrocher : To place on to a spit or skewer.

Emincer : To cut food into very thin slices.

Emmental Cheese (Sw.) : This hard, dull yellow cheese is made from the highest quality milk only. It has a distinctly nutty taste, and has large eyes the size of cherries. Suitable as a dessert or cooking cheese. Similar to gruyère.

Emulsion : A mixture of two varying liquids which do not readily combine with each other e.g. oil and water. However the mixture can be assisted by either a) vigorous shaking or beating, by hand or in an electric blender, as when making French dressing or mayonnaise, or b) adding emulsifying agents and stabilisers, such as albumin, agar, egg yolks or gums as in margarine, ice cream or salad cream. They are also used in baking to smooth the incorporation of fat into the dough, and to keep the crumbs soft.

En Croute : Food encased in pastry before cooking.

Endive : See Chicory.

Endive Stumps : See Chicory Gourilos.

Endosperm : The starchy substance of a grain.

English Bean : See Broad Bean.

English Mustard : A useful ground spice which can be purchased already 'made-up' in a jar, But is better and more versatile when used in powder form, that can be made into a paste if required by simply adding a little cold water. Do not use vinegar, boiling water or salt as these will destroy the enzymes and make it bitter rather than hot. The powder can be added to recipes as required like any other spice. Mainly used with chicken or beef dishes.

En Papillote : Food wrapped, cooked and served in oiled or buttered paper or foil.

Ensete : See Banana, False.

Entrecôte : A cut of meat from the middle part of the loin, or from between the rib bones of beef. Normally grilled.

Entrée : Third course in a formal meal, following the fish or main course, or in America it is the name of the main course.

Entremet : Sweet, pudding or dessert course of a main meal.

Enzymes : Present in all fresh foods, most of which are killed by cooking.

Epaule de (Fr.) : A French term for 'the shoulder of' e.g. lamb or pork.

Epicarp : See Zest.

Épigramme : Dish comprising breast and cutlets of lamb egg-and-crumbed, then grilled or fried.

Epinards (Fr.) : French name for spinach.

Eplucher : To peel.

Epoisses Cheese (Fr.) : A soft round cheese with an orange crust, made from curdled milk and sometimes flavoured with black pepper, clove or fennel, then soaked in wine or brandy. Can be eaten either fresh or ripe.

Epsom Salts : (Magnesium Sulphate). Used as a purgative.

Érythrin : A group of thick, rounded fish with excellent flesh, cooked as bass (sea perch).

Escalope : Thin slice of meat usually veal, or fish which is beaten flat and shallow-fried, often in butter, after crumbing. It sometimes refers to portions of fish.

Escargo : See Snail.

Esculade: See Manna.

Espagnole : A classical basic rich brown sauce, made from ham, veal and partridge. Often used as a basis for many other brown sauces.

Essence : Generally, the highly flavoured oily extract of a whole variety of foodstuffs used to enhance many food preparations. See also Extract.

Estouffade : Clear brown stock, generally used to dilute various other sauces.

Estragon : An alternative name for tarragon.

Ewe : Female sheep whose meat is prepared and cooked as mutton.

Expeller Cake : The residue of oil seeds such as cotton, coconut, groundnut, sesame, sunflower etc., after the oil has been removed by pressing, which is itself pressed into 'cakes'. A valuable source of protein.

Extract : A concentrated flavouring produced by evaporating the whole of various malt, meat, and vegetable juices. See individual names for details. See also Essence.

Extra Virgin Olive Oil : Made from the first pressing of olives, and is therefore the most expensive and also the best. It is thick, green, and has a powerful flavour. Use for vinaigrettes, mayonnaise, and cooking vegetables.

Eyes : Describes the holes formed in cheese during its natural fermentation.

Fadge : Irish potato bread.

Faggot : Small savoury cake made of pork offal, onion and breadcrumbs, which is usually baked. Also an old name for a small bunch of herbs tied with string and used for flavouring. Now known as bouquet garni.

Fahrenheit : A scale of temperature, where the freezing point of water is 32^0 F and the boiling point is 212^0 F.

Falafels : Savoury rissoles originating from the Middle East. Made of white beans, haricot or chick peas, heavily spiced and deep fried.

False Oats : Variety of oats.

Farce : See Forcemeat.

Farci : A French term meaning 'stuffing'.

Farfalle (It.) : Bows of pasta made in all sizes.

Farfals : Ground, granulated or shredded alimentary paste or pasta.

Farina : A general term for starch. In U.K. it means potato starch, in U.S. it means wheat starch or durum starch (semolina).

Farinaceous : Refers to foods that contain a high starch content such as cereals, potatoes and certain pulses.

Farina Dolce (It.) : Fine flour made from wheat, nuts or potatoes or just dried chestnuts.

Farle : Round, flat oatmeal cake baked on a griddle.

Farm Cheese : Cottage cheese that has had the curd pressed.

Faséole (Fr.) : Variety of haricot bean.

Fast Foods : Quick-cook production lines like burgers, pizzas, chicken and sandwiches.

Fats : Substances that are insoluble in water, but are in organic solvents.

Fava Bean : See Broad Bean.

Favanti : See Maccaroncelli.

Faverolles : French name for haricot beans.

Fawn : Young deer.

Fecula : A name for foods that are almost entirely starch, prepared from roots and stems by grating such as tapioca, sago and arrowroot.

Fecule : See Potato flour.

Feet : Normally associated with pig's trotters, although cow's heel and calf's foot are also feet. See individual headings for description and uses.

Fennel : (Cummin Sweet, Anethum). A perennial plant, where the fresh leaves are used chopped, in mayonnaise, salads, soups, vegetables and vinaigrette sauces, or cooked with roast lamb, mutton or oily fish. A good substitute for dill. Do not confuse with the vegetable florence fennel.

Fennel Pear : (Fenowlet). Variety of pear with a slight flavour of aniseed.

Fennel Seed : Are ideal with roast pork and chicken, having a similar flavour to celery with a slight aniseed taste, and can be used in a wide range of dishes from apple pies to curries.

Fenugreek (Ind.) : (Methi). These small flat brownish-beige seeds are essential in curries, but because of their slightly bitter flavour, should be used sparingly. They are especially good in fish curries, where the whole seeds are gently fried at the start of cooking; they can also be ground and added to curry powders. The green leaves are used in Indian cooking and when spiced (ground), the bitter taste is quite piquant and acceptable. The plant is very easy to grow from the seed, identical to mustard and cress, and when at the two-leaf stage, it makes a tangy addition to salads.

Féra : A north European freshwater variety of salmon with a very delicate flavour.

Fermentation : A term used to describe the activity of live enzymes changing the consistency of previously mixed ingredients, either solid or liquid e.g. bread, cakes, yoghurt, wine etc.

Fermented Milk : Milk from various types of animal that has been fermented by adding bacteria and yeast, when the lactose is converted to lactic acid, and in some instances to alcohol. There are many variations of this commodity, including cieddu, dadhi, kuban and yoghurt.

Fermiere (Fr.) : Prepared and cooked in the Farmhouse style i.e. with a garnish of carrots, cauliflower, fried potatoes and lettuce.

Fetta Cheese (Grk) : A Greek semi-soft curd cheese made from ewes' milk. It is white and very salty.

Fettuccini (It.) : Long strands of wide egg noodles.

Feuilletage (Fr.) : Flaky puff pastry.

Fiatole : Flat, broad fish with delicate flesh. Cook as turbot.

Fibre : In dietary terms, it is the structural parts of plant tissues which are not (or only partly) digested by humans, which includes cellulose, pectin and gums. Used to be known as roughage or bulk. Crude fibre is indigestible residue after several extractions from a substance.

Fidelini (It.) : The finest type of spaghetti which is normally bought 'nested'.

Field Beans : (British field beans). The only bean native to England. Smaller than broad beans, and normally white, the outer skin can be tough, so they are best liquidised and sieved into soups - or at least used in a recipe where they are blended first in a vegetable mill and then added to the rest of the dish.

Figs : Can be green or purple in colour, and bought fresh, dried or canned. Fresh ripe figs should yield evenly under gentle pressure, and are delicious eaten on their own, with yoghurt or cream. Dried, canned or unripe figs, can be stewed, and used in cakes, jams or pickles. Very high in dietary fibre.

Filbert : Variety of hazel nut, which is flask-shaped and should be completely covered by firm husks. See Hazelnut.

Filet Mignon : A very small fillet of beef.

Fillet : The undercut of the sirloin of pork, beef or veal. Also used to describe the boned breasts of poultry, or boned and sliced portions of fish.

Filo Paste : A thin strudel dough. Comes in long packages consisting of paper-thin sheets of dough dusted with flour, stacked, and folded up. Keep refrigerated or frozen.

Findon Haddock : See Finnan Haddock.

Fine Granulated Sugar : See Castor Sugar.

Fines Herbes (Fr.) : Mixture of finely chopped fresh parsley, chervil, tarragon and chives.

Fining Agents : Substances used to clarify liquid by precipitation, e.g. albumin, isinglass and gelatine.

Finnan /Findon Haddock : Smoked haddock that has been left on the bone.

Fino : Dry Sherry, substituted for rice wine in stir fry.

Finocchio : See Florence Fennel.

Firkin : A quarter size barrel of beer, i.e. 9 gallons.

Fish : A major source of nutritious food, which is easily digestible. However, all fish must be very fresh when prepared and cooked. When purchasing, there must be firm flesh, a clean fresh smell and bright clear eyes and scales, and fresh red gills.

Fish Ham (Jap.) : Red fish like tuna and marlin that is pickled, then mixed with whale and pork fat.

Fish Kettle : An oval or oblong pan with a lid and an inner detachable grid for poaching fish.

Fish Paste : A spread made from ground fish and cereal.

Fish Sauce (Ind.) : A thin salty, brown sauce made from the liquid drained from small variety of fish packed in wooden barrels with salt. Can be substituted by a mixture of light soy sauce and dried shrimp paste.

Five-Spice Powder : A coffee-coloured aromatic seasoning, consisting of star anise, szechuan pepper, fennel, cloves, and cinnamon. It is very strong and pungent, and only a pinch or a ¼ teaspoon is required to season 1-2 lbs of meat or poultry. Used extensively in Chinese cooking.

Flageolet Beans : (Green Shell Beans). These are very young French beans, picked from the pod when very young and tender. Very popular in France, adds a subtle taste to a salad or hot dish. Available fresh or canned. Can be substituted by Lima beans.

Flake : Separating cooked food, normally fish into individual flaky slivers, or, grating chocolate or cheese into small slivers.

Flake-Fish : See Huss.

Flakes : A general name given to cereals that have been flattened and processed in a mill.

Flaky Pastry : See Puff Pastry.

Flamande : In the Flemish style, with a garnish of braised cabbage and other mixed vegetables.

Flambé (Fr.) : Flamed; e.g. food tossed in a pan to which burning brandy or other alcohol is added.

Flamber : To singe game or poultry after plucking to remove any small remaining feathers

Flan : A culinary term used to describe round, flat pastry cases, normally having a savoury or sweet filling.

Flap Jacks : Crisp cakes made from rolled oats, fat and sugar. Normally served with honey or syrup.

Flatten : In culinary terms, to beat flatter a cut of meat with a mallet to tenderise it, which will also simplify certain cooking operations.

Flatulance : The production of gas in the intestines.

Flavouring : To enhance the taste of foods by the addition of herbs, spices and other commodities, either during or after the preparation and cooking operations of that food. See also seasoning.

Fleurons : Small shaped pieces of rolled puff pastry, fried or baked until golden brown, and served as croûtons, with soups or entrées.

Flint Corn : Very hard grained variety of maize.

Flitch : A side of bacon with the leg removed, and then boned.

Florence Fennel : (Finocchio). This vegetable from the *Celeriac* family, which looks like a root, is the swollen stem bases with the top leaves removed. It has a distinct aniseed flavour. Choose well-rounded roots, of pale green to white colour, avoiding any which are deep green. Available all year round. Use sliced raw in salads, or boiled as a vegetable. Do not confuse with the herb, fennel.

Florence Oil : High grade olive oil.

Florentine : Of fish and eggs; served on a bed of buttered spinach and coated with cheese sauce, or thin petit-four biscuit made of nuts, glace fruit and chocolate.

Flounder : (Fluke). A flat fish which can be cooked whole or filleted, and used in place of brill, dab, plaice or turbot. Cook as plaice.

Flour : Generally refers to ground or milled wheat used in bread-making, but also means rye, oatmeal, corn, rice, potato or other cereal flour.

Flute : Culinary term for cutting fruit or vegetables in a decorative manner to enhance the presentation of many varied dishes.

Flûte (Fr.) : The popular long French loaf or roll.

Foie Gras (Fr.) : The preserved liver of specially prepared and flattened geese or ducks.

Folding In : Enveloping one light ingredient or mixture such as flour or whisked egg whites into another heavier mixture, using a large metal spoon or spatula, and continually folding one into the other until thoroughly blended.

Foncer : To line the bottom of a pan or casserole dish with thin slices of ham or bacon.

Fondant : Minute sugar crystals suspended in a sugar syrup. Used as a creamy filling in chocolates, biscuits and for decorating cakes. Made by boiling a sugar solution with confectioners glucose, then cooling rapidly while continuously stirring.

Fondue (Sw) : Melted cheese and white wine dish into which diners dunk cubes of bread or meat cubes until cooked to their taste. Usually performed using long pronged fondue forks.

Fontina Cheese (It.) : A soft, fat cheese from Northern Italy, slightly straw-coloured and has a few small holes. The orange-coloured rind is often thicker than on other cheeses.

Food : Any substance taken in by mouth to maintain life and growth i.e. for energy building and replacing tissue.

Fool : Cold dessert consisting of fruit puree and whipped cream or custard.

Forcemeat : (Farce) Highly seasoned stuffing made from veal, pork or sausage plus onions and herbs. Derived from Farci - French for Stuffing.

Forcing Bag : (Piping Bag) A funnel-shaped cotton or nylon bag with various shaped nozzles through which creamy mixtures can be piped into designs.

Foreleg of Ham : (Picnic Ham). The cut of meat below the ham or shoulder of both the fore and hind legs of a pig.

Fourme (Fr.) : A sharp, blue-veined cheese, shaped like a drum, crumbly, and slightly salty.

Fourre : A preparation coated with sugar or cream.

Fovantini : See Maccaroncelli.

Frankental (GER) : (Black Hamburg). A variety of very large, black juicy grapes.

Frankfurters : Sausages made from cured meat which is then smoked and cooked.

Frappé (Fr.) : Iced or set on a bed of ice.

Frapper : To chill with ice. Normally refers to champagne.

Freeze : To reduce the temperature of a liquid or substance until ice is formed or turns to a solid state due to the temperature.

Freeze-Drying : Fast freezing food in a high vacuum which removes the formed ice as vapour without melting. With this method of freezing, there is no loss of flavour or texture.

Freezing : Solidifying or preserving food by chilling or storing it at 0° C, (32° F).

French Beans : (Dwarf, Snap, Stringer, Kidney or Kenya Beans). A variety of Green Beans varying from almost flat pods up to 5 inches long to short plump beans. Most varieties are stringless and are cooked and eaten whole in their pods. Available fresh or canned. When more mature, but still green and fresh, the beans only are eaten - see Flageolot Beans, and when fully mature and then dried they are cooked and eaten as pulses - see Haricot Beans, or processed to produce baked beans. A very versatile and widely used bean.

French Dressing : A temporary emulsion of oils and acid supporting herbs and flavourings, which can be revived as required by shaking. It is sometimes stabilised by the addition of Pectin or Vegetable Gum.

Frenching : Breaking up fibres of meat into pieces by cutting diagonally, or criss-cross.

French Spinach (U.S.) : See Orach.

Fricadelles (Fr.) : Meat balls, made with minced pork and veal, spices white breadcrumbs, cream and egg; poached in stock or shallow-fried.

Fricassé (Fr.) : White stew of chicken, rabbit, veal and vegetables which are first fried in butter, then cooked in stock and finished with cream and egg yolks.

Frijole Bean : See Pinto Bean.

Fritters : (Beignets). Generally describes any item of food that is dipped in batter, then deep-fried. It is also used to describe pastry or dough pockets filled with various preparations, and then deep-fried. See also Waffles.

Frog : A delicacy, but only the legs are edible.

Frog Fish : See Angler.

Fromage (Fr.) : The French word for Cheese.

Frost : To coat a cake with an icing of confectioners sugar, or to dip the rim of a glass in egg white and caster sugar, and then chill in a refrigerator until set.

Frothing : Dredging the surface of roast meat or poultry with flour and browning in a hot oven.

Fructarian : A form of vegetarian diet containing only foods that can be picked while leaving the parent plant to flourish. This includes fruits, nuts and some vegetables.

Fructose : (Fruit Sugar). A sugar, slightly different to cane or beet sugar, that is found in fruit juices, honey and flower nectar. In recent years, it has become available in powder form or syrup to be used as a substitute for ordinary sugar, and is believed to have a nutritional value.

Fruit : Botanically, it is any fleshy, seed-bearing part of a plant, but in many cases, 'fruits' of several types of plants are classed as vegetables. During ripening, starch turns to sugar, thus producing a sweet taste. Fruits are normally high in potassium and vitamin C.

Fruit Sugar : See Fructose.

Frumenty : Porridge made from wheat flour.

Frying : Cooking food on a hob in hot fat or oil. Can be either shallow fried in a pan with a little oil, or deep fried, where the food is totally immersed in a deep container of oil. This method of cooking normally results in a smaller loss of extractives than roasting.

Fudge : Caramel in which crystallisation of the sugar content has been induced by the addition of fondant.

Ful Medames : A small light brown bean, common in Egypt, are a tasty addition to soups, casseroles, salads and other savoury dishes. High in fibre.

Fumet (Fr.) : Concentrated broth or stock obtained from meat, fish or vegetables. Used to provide body to various sauces.

Fungi : Plants without differentiation into root, stem and leaf, such as mushrooms, truffles, woodears (Chinese black fungus) or Japanese matsutake. Bad fungi can seriously deteriorate food, but certain types are essential in the process of making Cheese.

Furcellaran : Danish agar used extensively as a gelling agent.

Furred Game : Applies to wild animals other than birds, that are hunted and eaten. This term includes hare, rabbit and venison, which, apart from rabbit, is best when hung by the feet for one or two weeks.

Fusilli (It.): Twisted macaroni with a hole through the centre. Considered to be the ultimate in spaghetti making.

Gaffelbitar : Semi-preserved herring in a high 12% salt content, as anchovies.

Galangal Greater (Ind.) : (Laos Powder). A rhizome like ginger with a delicate flavour. The flesh beneath the thin brown skin is creamy white. Prepare and use as ginger when required. Also available ground.

Galangal Lesser (Ind.) : (Aromatic Ginger). Although it is a member of the same family, it must not be substituted for ginger or vice versa. It is used only in certain dishes, and gives a pronounced aromatic flavour. When fresh, it is sliced or pounded to a pulp. Available dried in slices which must be pulverised before use, or in powdered form. It has an orange-red hue.

Galantine (Fr.) : Dish of boned and stuffed poultry, game or white meat glazed with aspic jelly and served cold.

Galette (Fr.) : A flat, round, flaky pastry cake traditionally baked for twelfth night, or a flat cake of sliced or mashed potato.

Gall : In culinary terms, the liquid secreted by liver.

Gallon : 1 Imperial Gallon = 4.546 Litres, 1 U.S. Gallon = 3.785 Litres.

Gambra : Type of partridge and cooked as such.

Game : Wild animals and birds which are hunted and eaten. For roasting and grilling, all game should be young - a condition that is more easily recognised when unplucked or still furred. The beak and/or feet should be pliable, the plumage or fur soft, and the breast plump. See also Game birds and Furred Game.

Game Birds : Before cooking, all game birds must be hung in order to tenderise the flesh and improve the 'gamey' flavour. They should be hung, unplucked and undrawn, by their beaks in a cool airy place, and are ready for cooking when the tail feathers can be easily plucked. The most common birds include pheasant, partridge, grouse and mallard.

Gammon : The hind leg of bacon pig, which has been cured while still part of the carcass.

Ganmodoki (Jap.) : Fried soybean curd and vegetables.

Gaper : A bivalve mollusc, cooked and eaten as cockles.

Gaperon/Gapron Cheese : A white buttermilk cheese, dry and piquant when ripe.

Garam Masala: A traditional blend of Indian herbs and spices, which are only added towards the end of the cooking to enhance the flavour as the qualities of the spices used are lost if excessively heated. It can really enhance a curry when sprinkled over the dish after cooking, as all the aromas are retained.

Garbanzo Beans: See Chick Peas.

Garden Cress : See Watercress.

Garden Orach : See Atriplex.

Garden Pea : See Pea.

Garfish : See Conger Eel.

Garlic: Available fresh as corms consisting of the cluster of bulbs which are pulled from the corm and used as required. Probably the most popular of all flavourings, and is also prized for its health-giving properties. It is very versatile, and with its pungent taste and smell it can be added to virtually any savoury dish according to taste. Also available ground for convenience but this does not compare with fresh bulbs. When stewed slowly, it develops a mild sweetness, but when fried to a nutty brown, it becomes more pungent with quite a 'bite' to it.

Garlic Butter : Butter blended with sieved crushed garlic.

Garlic Salt : This is simply basic salt with additives to give a slight flavour of garlic.

Garnishing : A major characteristic of French cuisine, which means to enhance the appearance of a dish by adding various edible decorations.

Garter Beans : See Green beans.

Gâteau : See Cake.

Gazpacho : Chilled soup with tomato, garlic, cucumber, peppers and vinegar.

Geans : Variety of black, red or white cherry with firm, fairly sweet flesh.

Gefillte /Gefultte Fish : German for stuffed fish.

Gel : A Solution or colloidal suspension that has set to jelly.

Gelatine : (Colle). A water-soluble transparent protein, made from animal bones and tissue, which melts in hot liquid and forms a jelly when cold. Used for sweet and savoury dishes.

Gelose : See Agar-Agar.

Genista : Pickled Broom buds which can be used as a substitute for Capers.

Genoa Cake : A rich fruit cake.

Génoise (Fr.) : A rich sponge cake made of eggs, sugar, flour and melted butter, layered, with various fillings added, and baked in a flat tin.

Germ : The embryo or sprouting part of a grain containing the vitamins and protein of which 80% is lost during refining, hence the beneficial advantage of using 'unrefined' grain products like wholewheat flour whenever possible.

Germon : A white species of tuna fish.

Gex (Fr.) : A pure white, blue-veined cheese.

Ghee (Ind.) : (Samna). Clarified butter, sold in tins, is pure butter-fat without any of the milk solids, made from the milk of the water buffalo or cow. It can be heated to much higher temperatures than normal butter, without burning, and imparts a distinctive flavour, used extensively in Asian recipes. Ideal for cooking, in place of ordinary butter - other than for pastry, mainly due to its distinctive aroma.

Gherkin : A small variety of warty cucumber grown specifically for pickling.

Giblets : Edible internal organs and trimmings of poultry and game, which include liver, heart, gizzard, neck, pinions, feet and cockscomb. Often used to enhance stews and soups.

Gigot : A name for a leg of lamb or mutton.

Gild : See Glaze.

Gill : Liquid measure equal to 1/4 pint or 5 fluid oz or 150ml.

Ginger : (Root Ginger). A rhizome with a unique and pungent flavour. Available as a fresh root or powdered. One should not be substituted for the other, as the fresh variety is far less 'spicy' than the dried ground form. In either form, it is used in both sweet and savoury dishes. Peeled and ground to a pulp, the fresh ginger is a popular ingredient in many curries; it is also available canned, crystalized in sugar, preserved in syrup, and used in ginger beer and ginger wine. Dried root ginger must be 'bruised with a rolling pin or hammer) before use, to open the fibres and help release the aromatic flavour. Ground ginger does not give the same flavour, and is mostly used in sweet dishes, desserts, creams, sauces, pickles and chutneys. It goes particularly well sprinkled on melons and peaches. See Preserved Ginger.

Ginkgo Nuts : (White Nuts). Used in soups and slow-cooked meat or poultry dishes, after being shelled and blanched. Also available in cans. Can be substituted by small new potatoes.

Ginnan (Jap.) : See Gingko nuts.

Gipsy Bread : A fruit bread containing black treacle.

Giraumont : West Indian pumpkin with sweet flesh. Can be cooked, or eaten raw in salads.

Girdle : See Griddle

Girella : A brightly-coloured scaleless sea-fish with fairly delicate flesh. Can be fried or stewed in a bouillabaisse.

Girole : A variety of fungi.

Gitana : A garnish whose main ingredient is onions.

Glaçagé : A culinary term used to describe various unrelated operations, namely, to :-
1. Glaze 2. Brown 3. Ice 4. Freeze.

Glacé (Fr.) : Glazed, frozen or iced.

Glacé de Viande (Fr.) : Meat glaze or residue in the bottom of a pan after frying or roasting meat, or concentrated meat stock.

Glasgow Magistrate : See Red Herring.

Glaze : (Gild). A glossy finish given to food by brushing with beaten egg, milk, sugar, syrup or jelly just after cooking, Then browning in oven.

Gloucester Cheese : There are two main varieties of this famous cheese. For descriptions, see Double, and Single Gloucester.

Glucose : (Dextrose, Grape or Blood Sugar). A form of sugar found naturally in plant tissues.

Glucose Syrup : (Confectioners Glucose, Corn or Starch Syrup). A humectant and a purified sweetening agent made from maize or potato starch. Used in sugar confectionary.

Gluten : A protein complex found in wheat and rye grains, which gives dough the viscid quality to retain gas when it rises, and helps to create different types of flours resulting in varying textures of bread, cakes and biscuits. It is not found in barley, maize or oats, which is useful when preparing gluten-free diets.

Glutinous Rice : (Sweet Rice, Sticky Rice). Oval-shaped cream grains, used for stuffings and as an ingredient in sweet dishes, and Oriental cooking. Must be soaked for at least 20 minutes before cooking. Like unwashed rice, it becomes sticky after cooking. Obtainable in most Chinese foodstores. Can be substituted by 'pudding rice'.

Glycerine /Glycerol : A humectant, and is a clear, colourless, odourless, sweet-tasting viscous liquid made from various fats, and used as a solvent for flavours, and as a moisture-retaining agent to slow down staling and drying out in certain breads and cakes.

Gnocchi (It.) : Small dumplings made from semolina, potatoes or choux pastry.

Goats' Beard : See Wild Salsify.

Goats' Milk : It has a sharper taste than cows milk and is a good substitute for those who are allergic to it. Also makes very good cheeses.

Gobo (Jap.) : See Burdock Root.

Goby : Very small fish with very delicate flesh. Normally eaten fried as gudgeon.

Godwit : A variety of marsh bird. Can be cooked as Woodcock.

Golden Berry : See Cape Gooseberry.

Golden Needles : (Lily buds). Long dried strips, golden in colour, and must be well soaked before cooking. They have a unique musty taste, and are best served when mixed with other ingredients such as meat or vegetables. Normally sold in bundles.

Golden Nugget : Despite its name, it is a member of the marrow or squash family.

Goma /Gomasia (Jap.) : (Sesame Salt). Made by grounding sesame seeds very finely, and then adding sea salt, (5 parts sesame to 1 part sea salt). Its nutty taste makes it a delicious addition to any savoury dish.

Good King Henry : (Wild Spinach). A very bitter green leaved plant, cooked as spinach.

Goose : Considered by many as the best of all poultry. A fatty bird with creamy-white flesh which cooks to a light brown, and has a slightly 'gamey' flavour. It serves less than a chicken, so allow 12-24oz. per person. Choose a bird with soft yellow legs and feet which still have a little down on them.

Gooseberry : A fruit that includes both culinary and dessert varieties, from fairly bitter to very sweet tasting. A semi-translucent fruit which often has a 'hairy' skin. Depending on variety, they are ideal in fruit salads, or for pie and tart fillings, or jam and jelly making. Avoid any squashy berries, or those with splits or blemishes to the skin.

Gorgonzola (It.) : A semi-hard yellowish -white cheese with blue veins.

Gosling : (Green Goose). A young goose not more than 6 months old.

Gouda Cheese : A creamy-tasting soft Dutch cheese with a high butter-fat content. This golden-yellow cheese is produced in squat moulds, and is not recommended for cooking.

Goujon (Fr.) : See Gudgeons.

Goulasch (Hung.) : (Gulyas). Beef and onion stew flavoured with tomato and paprika.

Gourd : (Cucurbits). Describes any vegetable of the *Cucurbitacaea* family, of which there are many varieties, such as cucumber, marrow, pumpkin, squash and melon. See also Dried Gourd strips.

Gourilos : See Chicory Gourilos.

Graham Bread : Loaves made from Graham flour. Graham cakes are made from Graham flour and milk.

Graham Flour : Fine ground wholewheat flour. Named after a famous miller, who promoted it in the U.S. See also Wholewheat Flour.

Graining : The crystallisation of sugar.

Grains : Available in various forms from whole unrefined grain to freeze-dried flakes, but the most used product is flour. The most common grains include barley, buckwheat, bulgar, corn, millet, oats, rye and wheat. See individual headings for descriptions and uses.

Grains of Paradise : An alternative name for cardamom seeds.

Gram Flour : (Besan flour, or Chickpea flour). Very fine quality yellow flour made from ground chickpeas, it has a good flavour and creamy texture, and is a popular ingredient of Indian cooking, especially when mixed with water to make a batter, for coating foods before frying, and for making soups and sauces. It should be sieved before use, and must be stirred vigorously to remove lumps. It is low in gluten and high in protein.

Granadilla : See Passion Fruit.

Granary Flour : A blend of wholewheat and rye flours with malted grains and caramel. As its constituents suggest, it has a slightly sweet malty flavour, and makes excellent unusual bread and pastry.

Granita (It.) : Half-frozen water ice.

Granites (It.) : A Sherbet with no meringue added.

Grape : Available all year round, and can be black/purple, green/white or red. The tiny seedless varieties are said to be the finest tasting. When buying, choose grapes that are firmly attached to their stems. Can be eaten raw, or in desserts and pies. They are available dried, in the form of currants, raisins or sultanas.

Grapefruit : A fruit available all year round, of which, there are several varieties:- white/yellow which is best for juicing, pink which is so sweet, it can be eaten like an orange, and red which is even sweeter. Most commonly served as a breakfast appetizer and a fruit juice drink, it is also used to make marmalade, or added to fruit salads, ices, cakes and desserts. It can also be baked or grilled.

Grape Leaves : See Vine leaves.

Grape Sugar : See Glucose.

Grass Jelly (Chin.) : A black jelly made from seaweed. It is sold canned in Chinese stores, and is used in sweet dishes in China, and parts of Southeast Asia.

Gratin (Fr.) : See au gratin.

Grating : Shaving vegetables, cheese or any hard food, using either a hand grater or blender attachment. See shredding.

Gravalax (Scand.) : Scandinavian dill-pickled salmon.

Gravenche : Variety of salmon and resembling Féra. Cook as Féra or trout.

Gravy : Juices exuded by roasted meat and poultry, or a sauce made from these juices by boiling with stock or wine, and sometimes thickened with flour.

Gravy Browning : A dark fluid made from burnt sugar, used to colour soups and sauces.

Grayling : A freshwater fish, similar to and cooked as trout.

Grease : To coat any cooking vessel with fat to prevent the food contents from sticking to the container.

Grecque, a la (Fr.) : Cooked in the Greek style, i.e. cooked in stock and olive oil, or dishes garnished with savoury rice and dressed with olive oil and vinegar.

Green Bacon : Bacon that has been cured in brine only, and is unsmoked. It does not keep as well as bacon that has been further cured by smoking.

Green Beans : (Haricot Vert or Flagelot). A complex family which includes many different varieties. Grown mainly for their pods, which are boiled, steamed, stir-fried or sauteed, either whole or sliced, (including the small inner pea seeds). The most common varieties, include:-, broad, french, lima, runner, snap, soya, kenya wax, drumstick, and garter beans, - a truely cosmopolitan vegetable. When bought, the pods should break with a crisp snap, and the insides should be fresh and juicy. Can be eaten hot or cold.

Greengage : A variety of plum with a slightly bitter flavour. Used for jams and pie fillings.

Green Goose : See Gosling.

Green Lentils : A variety of lentils.

Green Masala : A paste made from fresh (hence green) coriander, garlic, chillies and ginger. It forms an excellent and essential basis for Indian dishes such as biriani and korma.

Green Onions : See Scallions.

Green Pea : See Pea.

Green Pepper : See Capsicums.

Greens : See Cabbage.

Green Shell Bean (U.S.) : See Flagelot.

Green Snap Beans (U.S.) : Same as String bean. An American name for French beans.

Green Split Peas : Slightly more unusual than yellow split peas, so traditional in British cookery, but have the same faintly sweet flavour.

Grenadins : Small, triangular slices of veal fillet, interlaced with larding bacon.

Griddle : (Girdle). Flat iron plate, or shallow rimmed pan, used to bake pancakes, scones or cakes on top of the stove.

Grig : A small freshwater eel.

Grill : The contemporary form of a spit, where food is placed on the barred gridiron, and placed either above or below the source of heat. See Broiler.

Grillade : French for grilled food.

Grilling : (Broiling). Heating food either over or under a direct flame. Nowadays, food can be cooked to perfection in a very natural way.

Grilse : A young Salmon weighing about 4-8 lbs.

Grind : To reduce hard ingredients into small particles using either a mill, pistol and mortar or an electric grinder.

Grisette : Edible variety of mushroom.

Grissini (It.) : Long, slim, brittle breadsticks.

Gristle : The cartilage, or tough flexible tissue found in meat, which should be removed before in preparation before cooking.

Groats : De-husked grains, especially oats, often milled. See Embden or Scotch Groats.

Grog : Hot rum-based drink served with a slice of lemon and sugar.

Ground Nut : See Peanut.

Ground Oats : See Oatmeal.

Ground Rice : More granular than rice flour, and gives a crisper texture when used in batters or other mixtures.

Grouse : A popular game bird with delicate flesh, which when young, is normally roasted, and serves one person. Older birds, with rounded tips to their wings, are better when casseroled. Hang for about 3 days. Prepare and cook as pheasant.

Gruyère Cheese : A firm, pale, full-flavoured cheese from France/ Swiss region, with small eyes, and a crinkled, slightly greasy golden-brown rind. Excellent as a dessert or cooking cheese, and in fondues. Similar to Emmenthal.

Guarana : A dried paste made from the seeds of a South American climbing shrub, which is rich in caffeine, and is used as a beverage, similar to cocoa.

Guava : A tropical fruit which can be round or pear-shaped, and usually have yellow skins with pink flesh. Available fresh or canned. Having a slightly sharp taste, they can be eaten raw or stewed and preserved as guava jelly for use in tarts and fillings. When prepared to eat raw, use immediately, or sprinkle with lemon juice to prevent discoloration.

Gudgeons : (Goujon). Small fish that are normally fried and served as a garnish.

Gugelhupf (Ger.) : Sweetened yeast cake with dried fruit, baked in a fluted ring mould.

Guiche (Fr.) : From Alsace open tart with savoury filling based on eggs and cream. Equivalent to quiche.

Guinea Fowl : A game bird originally, but now bred. The flesh is firm and creamy-white with a slight flavour of pheasant. Suitable for braising, roasting or casseroles. Should be hung for several days.

Gula Jawa : See Palm Sugar.

Gula Malaka : See Palm Sugar.

Gulyas : See Goulasch.

Gum Arabic : (Acacia). A thickening agent or stabiliser made from the *Acacia* plant, used in jellies and confectionary, to prevent crystallisation, or as an emulsifier in sour or processed cheese.

Gumbo : See Okra.

Gums : Substances that can disperse in water to form viscous masses, obtained from either seeds from the arabic, guava or karaya seeds, or more commonly from seaweed such as agar or kelp. See Gum Arabic and Syrup Gum.

Gur : See Jaggery.

Gurnet : A saltwater fish often sold as red mullet. Commonly red, but also grey and yellow varieties. Firm, dry white flaky flesh, cooked whole or filleted.

Haddock : A round fish which is a superior member of the cod family. The roe is also considered to be a great delicacy, especially in France. The white flesh, which should be very firm, is sold either whole, or as steaks or fillets. Suitable for baking, frying, grilling or poaching. A very versatile high quality fish. See also Smoked Haddock.

Haggis : Savoury highly spiced Scottish dish, consisting of chopped offal, suet, onions and oatmeal, which is boiled in the stomach lining of a sheep.

Hake : (Colin). A long, white, round slender fish, similar to Cod with firm white flaky flesh, and almost boneless. Suitable for cooking whole or filleted, and can be prepared as cod.

Hakusai (Jap.) : See Chinese Cabbage.

Haldi : See Turmeric.

Half-glaze : A sauce combined with a jellied ingredient, used to mask savoury dishes.

Halibut : A large flat fish, normally sold in fillets or steaks. A strong flavoured fish, expensive, but distinctive flavour, and on the dry side. Available fresh or smoked.

Halibut Liver Oil : Oil extracted halibut, and is the richest natural source of from vitamin A.

Halumi Cheese : Similar to fetta cheese, but matures very quickly and should be eaten soon after purchase.

Halva : (Chalva, Halwa and Halowa). A Middle Eastern sweetmeat composed of an aerated mixture of glucose, sugar, and crushed sesame seeds.

Ham : The whole hind leg of a pig that has been removed from the carcass and cured. There are many different varieties and flavours, depending on the method of curing and whether it is subsequently 'smoked'.

Hamaguri (Jap.) : See Clams.

Hamburger (U.S.) : Minced meat patty which is fried or grilled and served in a soft round bun.

Hand of Pork : The fatty foreleg of a pig. Normally salted and boiled, or roasted.

Hanging : Suspending meat or game in a cool, dry place until it is tender.

Hard Roe : Eggs of the female fish, normally shallow-fried or grilled. See Roe.

Hard Sauce : Sweet butter sauce flavoured with brandy, rum or whisky, which is chilled until hard, then cut into cubes and served on hot puddings when it then melts.

Hare : There are two main types of this furred game, the English or brown hare, and the Scottish or blue hare. A young hare, known as a leveret weighing about 6-7lbs. should be hung for about one week, and are best roasted. Older hare are better casseroled.

Haricot Bean : (Boston Bean, Dry Shell Bean, Faverolles, Haricot Bean Sec, Navy Bean). Dried seeds of the French bean plant. The term usually refers to the large white dried French or haricot bean, or its smaller counterpart - pearl haricot which is used for making 'baked beans', and which is also a traditional ingredient of the French Cassoulet. However, the haricot family is very large and includes all the following:- bianco di spagna, black, black-eyed, borlotti, cannellini, flagelot, red kidney, and pinto beans, and probably a few more. See individual names for descriptions and uses.

Haricot Sec (Fr.) : See Haricot Bean.

Haricot Vert (Fr.) : Simply translates to green bean. Another name for young French beans.

Hash : Dish of leftover chopped meat, potatoes or other vegetables, which are fried together.

Hashi (Jap.) : Chopsticks.

Haslet : An old English name for a sausage made from pigs offal, seasoning and flour.

Hatelets : Small skewers used for securing ingredients for ornamental garnishes.

Haunch : Generally the hind quarter of the ox or deer.

Hazel-Grouse : A European variety of Grouse.

Hazel Nuts : (Cobnuts). Rich in oil, and normally sold loose in their shells for eating raw, or in packets, shelled, for use in butters, confections, desserts, chocolates and ice creams. Can also be roasted for use in specific recipes.

Hazelnut Oil : Cold pressed from ripe nuts, it is delicately flavoured and ideal for salads, mayonnaise, dressings and sauces. It is expensive and should be used sparingly, but if not a problem, then use as liberally as you would normal olive oil.

Heads : Normally pig's, or sheep's, but occasionally calf's, and are sold whole or halved. Can be used to make brawn, or as a base for broths or meat pie fillings.

Hearts : All hearts including calf, lamb, ox and pig make good nutritional eating, but require long slow cooking, by either braising or casseroling. Lamb's and calf's are the most tender, followed by pig and ox.

Henware : See Honeyware.

Herb : Normally refers to the whole of the soft-stemmed aromatic plant, and in this book, we are only concerned with the varieties grown for their fragrance, and not necessarily for their medicinal properties. In order to clarify the difference between herbs and spices, this book considers herbs to be the stems or leaves of the plant, either fresh or dried, whole or ground, and spices as the whole or ground seeds and/or pods of the plant.

Herbes de Provence : A blend of mild herbs with a typically Mediterranean flavour.

Herbs : Plants without a woody stem. Culinary herbs, which are available in fresh or dried form, include basil, bayleaf, chervil, marjoram, mint oregano, parsley, rosemary, sage, savory, tarragon and thyme. Used for their aromatic properties.

Herring : A small, delicately flavoured and bony salt-water fish, with a firm, brownish flesh. A very cheap nutritious fish, rich in proteins and vitamins A and D. Ideal for grilling, baking or barbecue. Available smoked or pickled. See Bismarck, Bloater, Buckling and Kipper.

Herring Roes : Long, almost sausage-shaped sacks of eggs of the herring fish, which can be either 'hard' or 'soft'. An ideal delicacy when grilled or fried, and eaten with toast and tomato sauce.

Hibachi (Jap.) : Earthenware or charcoal, brazier.

Highball : A long, cool iced, alcoholic drink, consisting of spirits, vermouth and a dilutant.

Hilsa : A fish, similar to, and cooked as mackerel.

Hing (Ind.) : See Asafoetida.

Hiziki (Jap.) : A thin, shredded-looking seaweed used as a vegetable.

Hog : The name for a male pig.

Hogget : A one year old sheep.

Hogs, Fat : Fat that covers the pigs' kidneys and fillets. Used in forcemeats and black puddings.

Hogshead : A double-size barrel of beer equivalent to 72 gallons.

Hoisin Sauce (Chin.) : A thick brownish- red spicy soy and vegetable based sauce made from vegetables. Used for flavouring shellfish, duck, spare ribs and vegetables. Sold in jars or cans.

Hollandaisse : Hot egg yolk and butter sauce, normally served with eggs, fish, vegetables and salads. Similar to a well seasoned mayonnaise.

Homard (Fr.) : French name for lobster.

Hominy : Prepared coarsely ground maize kernels that have had the germ and pericorp removed by soaking in caustic soda.

Honey : The most ancient form of sweetener. Use in preference to sugar in certain recipes, but do not be deceived by its cariogenic properties. There are many varieties, and the taste, colour and composition quality depends largely on the area and variety of flowers from which the bees collect their nectar, which produces this syrupy liquid.

Honeydew Melon : A yellow-skinned variety of melon, with sweet, juicy flesh, and probably the tastiest and most popular variety of this type of fruit. When ripe, it should yield slightly when gently pressed around the stem end.

Honeyware : (Henware) A variety of seaweed, which is normally boiled or pickled.

Hoop Cheese : See Baker's Cheese.

Hops : The female flower of the *Humulus Lupulus* plant, which contains bitter resins and essential oils for brewing beers.

Horned Melon : See Kiwano.

Hors-d'oevres (Fr.) : Hot or cold delicate appetisers served at the start of a meal, which like garnishes, are a speciality of France and a culinary science in their own right.

Horse Bean : See Broad Bean.

Horse Mackerel : See Saurel. Also, an American name for a species of tuna.

Horse Mushrooms : Large field mushrooms whose flesh turns brown when bruised or cut during food preparation.

Horseradish : A root vegetable which is grated and used as a flavouring. Although the flavour is very pungent, it is completely destroyed by cooking, and should therefore never be added to hot dishes. It is mainly used as a condiment, or flavouring in mayonnaise, or freshly grated, as a garnish to salads. It is also available dried, but must be reconstituted before use.

Hotbreads (U.S.) : American term for waffles and pancakes.

Hotch-Potch : Generally used to describe a thick meat stew or soup.

Hot Water (Pastry) : (Raised Crust) A paste which includes fat, and is combined with hot water, and used for topping raised pies.

Hramsa : A soft Scottish cheese, made from double cream, and flavoured with wild garlic. A good dessert cheese.

Huckleberry : See Bilberry.

Hulling: Removing green calyx from strawberries and raspberries, or the pods from peas or broad beans.

Humble Pie : See Umbles.

Humerant : A substance that absorbs moisture, e.g. glucose syrup and glycorene, which are used to maintain the water content in baked products to prevent staling or dryness. They also allow the addition of sugar to a mixture without needing any more water, which helps to prevent mould growth.

Hummus : Probably the most popular 'vegetable' puree in the world, with its marvellous earthy flavour of cooked chick peas blended with olive oil, garlic and tahini. There are many variations to this basic recipe.

Hungarian Pepper : See Paprika.

Hung Beef : Beef that is hung for about 3 weeks until dry, then salted and rolled to preserve it. Sometimes smoked.

Husk /Hull : The outer woody cellulose covering of cereal grain, which is high in fibre content.

Huss : (Dogfish, Rigg or Rock Eel). A boneless fish with sweet, flaky but firm flesh, suitable for most methods of cooking, and normally sold already skinned. Reputedly a member of the shark family.

Hussarde : Hollowed tomatoes, filled with finely grated onions and horseradish.

Hyacinth Bean : See Lablab Bean.

Hydrolyse : To split and change a substance by a natural chemical reaction, for example, when grain is hydrolysed the starch is changed into maltose (malt sugar) and other minor substances, and proteins are converted into various amino acids.

Hyssop : A pungent, aromatic herb whose oil from the leaves is used mainly in the production of liqueurs.

Iceberg : Large, firm compact lettuce, which stays crisp well, especially when refrigerated.

Ice Cream : A frozen confection made from fat milk solids and sugar, the flavour and texture of which depends largely on the percentage of fat milk solids that it contains, which varies greatly, mainly according to the country of origin.

Icing : Sweet coating for cakes made from specially processed very fine sugar, known commercially as 'icing sugar' plus other various ingredients dependant on the recipe. Can be used dry, sprinkled on cakes and pastries as a decoration.

Idli : A mixture of cooked rice and black gram, which is fermented. A dish from the Far East.

Imperial : Variety of plum.

Imperiale : A very large wine bottle used for storing and maturing wines such as claret. Or, a garnish of foie gras, mushrooms, truffles and quenelles.

Improving : An alternative term for Age ing.

Incising : Cutting diagonal slits in fish before grilling or frying to assist the cooking process.

Indian Corn : See Maize.

Indian Cress : (Nasturtium) A variety of cress, whose leaves and flowers are used in salads, and the seeds can be used as a substitute for capers.

Indian Date : See Tamarind.

Indian Fig : See Prickly Pear.

Indian Gram : An Indian name given to small dried peas, e.g. green gram, red gram, black gram.

Indian Gooseberry : See Emblic.

Indian Nut : See Pine Nut.

Indian Pea : See Petit Pois.

Infuse : To steep in herbs, tea leaves, coffee, water, milk or other liquid to extract the flavours.

Interlarding : See Larding.

Intestines : Used to describe the whole of the gastro-intestinal tract after the stomach i.e. the small and large intestines.

Inversion : Applied to sucrose, it means to revert back to fructose and glucose.

Invert Sugar : Produced by the inversion of sucrose, and is 30% sweeter than normal sugar. Used mainly in making confectionary to prevent crystallisation.

Irish Coffee : Coffee flavoured with Irish whiskey and topped with thick cream.

Irish Moss : See Carrageen.

Irish Stew : Mutton cooked in white stock, with onions and potatoes.

Irlandaise (Fr.) : In the Irish style i.e. dishes, mainly stews, that always contain potatoes.

Iron : An essential mineral to maintain good health, and prevent anaemia. Found in meat, green vegetables, salads, cheese and eggs.

Isinglass : A precipitate of specially prepared ground protein membrane from the swim bladder of the sturgeon fish. Used to clarify liquids, especially beer, to carry down any suspended particles, which are mainly yeast, which then becomes the sediment. Can be substituted with gelatine.

Italian Marrow : See Courgette.

Italian Rice : See Arborio.

Italian Pastes : See Pasta.

Italienne (Fr.) : Usually denotes that macaroni is served as part of the main course.

Jackfruit : A tropical fruit with a very spiny, porcupine like appearance, that grows on the trunk and large boughs of trees. The flesh is similar to a very sweet plum, and is normally eaten raw. The seeds are also edible.

Jaffa Orange : A large thick-skinned sweet very juicy orange, almost seedless, and is probably the most popular of dessert oranges

Jaggery : Coarse dark sugar, made from either the sap of the *Coconut* palm, or raw cane sugar juice. Used as a sweetening agent, and to prevent rancidity of fats.

Jam : A non-citrus fruit preserve set to a gel. Can be used as a spread, or pie filling. See also Marmalade.

Jamaican Pepper : See Allspice.

Jambalayah : A Creole breakfast dish consisting of rice with ham or pork.

Jambon : Describes ham dishes cooked in pastry.

Japanese Bunching Onion : See Welsh Onion.

Japanese Horseradish (Jap.) : See Wasabi.

Japanese Medlar : See Loquats.

Japanese Radish : See Daikon.

Jap Cakes : Small brittle cakes made from sugar, egg-whites and almonds.

Jardinière, a la (Fr.) : Garnish of fresh spring vegetables, or small pieces of cooked vegetables, arranged in separate groups.

Jarret : A knuckle of veal or mutton.

Jarret of Pork : Pickled pig's trotters, boiled and served with sauerkraut.

Jasmine : Scented herb used in Oriental cooking and confectionary.

Jaunemange : A thick custard containing eggs which is set in moulds. See also blancmange.

Jeera : See Cumin.

Jelly : A colloidal suspension that has set. May be made from gelatin, pectin or agar, with natural fruit juice or synthetic flavouring added. Also describes clear meat or fish stocks which solidify when cold. American term for jam.

Jeraboam : The name for a double magnum of champagne.

Jerusalem Artichoke : See Artichoke.

Jesse : A bony freshwater fish that turns yellow when cooked. Prepare and cook as carp.

Jigger : An American term for a measure of spirits, about 1½ fluid oz..

John Dory : Oval, flat excellently flavoured fish, with firm white flesh, cooked as cod or turbot. The carcass is ideal for stock.

Johnny Cakes : Sweet buns made from flour, sugar, butter, eggs, yeast and candied peel. They are a derivation of 'Journey Cakes', which were baked for men travelling on long journeys.

Joint : Prime cut of meat for roasting, or to divide meat, game or poultry into individual pieces by dissecting at the joints.

Jordan Almond : The finest variety of almond.

Jugged: Meat dishes, such as jugged hare, which are stewed very slowly, in a covered pot until very tender and dark brown in colour.

Juice : Generally the liquid squeezed from fruit, or the residues of roast meats.

Jujube : The fruit of the Chinese date, which can be eaten raw, but is normally candied.

Julep (U.S.) : American name for a sweet drink.

Julienne : Vegetables or fruit rind cut into very thin, match-size strips and used as a garnish or an ingredient of certain recipes. Also, a clear vegetable soup.

Jumbles : Small lemon flavoured cakes.

Juniper Berry : These ripe berries are used as a flavouring in dishes such as sauerkraut, preserves, pickles and chutneys. Available fresh or dried.

Junket : A dessert made by precipitating milk with rennet, and discarding the whey.

Jus (Fr.) : Juices from roasting meat used as gravy, or as an ingredient for its sauce.

Jus Lie : A stock made from thickened and seasoned meat juices.

Kaffir Corn (Ind.) : An Indian variety of millet.

Kaffir Lime Leaves : Usually sold dried and should be soaked before use. Can be substituted with fresh citrus leaves.

Kagne : A variety of vermicelli.

Kakayo : See Cocoa.

Kaki : (Persimmon or Sharon Fruit). Lovely tomato-shaped fruit, with a slightly peachy flavour. See Persimmon.

Kale : (Borecole). It is the most hardy variety of the Brassica family. It is a very tasty green vegetable, but the leaves must be picked when young and tender, as the older leaves tend to become bitter. Rich in iron and vitamin C. Do not overcook.

Kalonji (Ind.) : See Black Onion Seeds.

Kaltschale (Russ.) : A fruit salad covered with chilled wine, liqueurs and syrups.

Kamaboko (Jap.) : Steamed fish cake.

Kandalla : See Eddoe.

Kanpyo (Jap.) : Dried gourd strips used to flavour dishes or for tying around small bundles of seaweed.

Kanten (Jap.) : See Agar-Agar.

Karashi (Jap.) : Mustard.

Karaya Gum : A form of Stabiliser.

Karella : A member of the gourd family. See also Bitter Lemon.

Kasha (Russ.) : Dry-roasted buckwheat.

Katemfe : An intensively sweet African fruit.

Katsuobushi (Jap.) : Dried bonito fish, which is a member of the tuna family. Used for flavouring, and a main ingredient of dashi - a basic Japanese stock.

Kebab (Turk.) : Marinated cubes of meat, fish, and/or vegetables, cooked on a skewer under a grill or on a barbecue or rotisserie.

Kedgeree : (Kitcheree). Breakfast or lunch dish of cooked fish rice and eggs. Also an Indian dish of rice, split pulses, onions and eggs.

Kéfir : A slightly alcoholic drink made from fermented cow or goat milk.

Kelp : Any type of large brown seaweed that comes from the species of *Genus Laminaria.*

Kemeri Nut : See Candle Nut.

Kenya Beans : See French Beans.

Kernels : The hard edible centres of most nuts.

Kern Milk : Scottish name for Buttermilk.

Ketchup : (Catsap). A spicy sauce or condiment made with the juice of fruit and/or vegetables, vinegar and spices.

Ketjap Manis : An Indonesian sweetened soy sauce.

Ketmie : See Okra.

Kewra : See Screwpine.

Kickshaws : A term from the French *Quelque Chose* - 'something', used to describe small dishes of delicate food

Kid : Young goat, slaughtered before weaning. The dry meat should be frequently basted during roasting.

Kidney : A very underrated source of nourishment. They vary in tenderness and texture according to the origin. Calf's and lamb's kidneys are the most tender, and ideal for grilling or frying. The coarser pig's kidney may also be grilled or fried, but for a longer period. Ox kidney is really only suitable for stewing or slow cooking.

Kidney Bean (U.S.) : See Red Bean.

Kilkis : Norwegian anchovies.

Kingfish : Large seafish with firm, white flesh. Prepare and cook as tuna.

Kipper : The most common type of cold-smoked herring. It is split and put into brine before being smoked. The flesh should be soft to the touch. Available whole, or in fillets, fresh or frozen.

Kirsch : Strong flavoured liqueur made from ripe cherries and used in various dessert dishes and confectionary.

Kitcheree (Ind.) : A savoury dish made from rice and lentils. An original form of kedgeree.

Kiwano (Africa) : A vine fruit originating in tropical Africa. It is cucumber-shaped, and at it's ripest, it is orange-yellow in colour with green pulp. It has a subtle taste of banana and lime mixed, and is delicious eaten raw, chilled on its own, but can be added to any fruit salad or drink cocktail.

Kiwi Fruit : (Chinese gooseberry). They have a sweet distinctive flavour, and can be eaten raw on their own, whole, or sliced and added to fruit salads or desserts. Their beautiful green flesh, which envelop the dark brown seeds, make a fantastic garnish to many sweet or savoury dishes. When buying, look for undamaged fruits which yield evenly to gentle pressure. The hairy light-brown skin must be removed before using. They keep well in the refrigerator.

Klipfish (Nor) : (Bacalao). Boned cod fish which is stored in salt for about a month, washed, and then slowly dried.

Kneaded Butter : Softened butter mixed with flour, and used to thicken soups, stocks, and sauces.

Kneading : Working elasticated dough to produce a good mix of ingredients.

Knobs : Small shellfish, similar to whelks.

Knotted Marjoram : The sweetest and most fragrant variety of marjoram.

Knuckle : The fleshy muscle of mutton leg, or the part of the leg between the 'ham' or shoulder, and the foot. An excellent joint for stews and pies. The bone provides a good flavour for many soups.

Kohlrabi : The thickened stem of a vegetable related to the cabbage family, which can be either green or purple. It has a delicate turnip-like flavour, and can be eaten raw in salads, or blanched, braised, boiled, steamed or sauteed. Remove twiggy stems before use.

Kombu (Jap.) : A variety of Japanese kelp or seaweed with broad, blackish-grey ribbons.

Konnyaku (Jap.) : Small gelatinous cakes made from flour of the tuberous roots of a vegetable known as Devil's Tongue. Normally sold canned.

Koofthas (Ind.) : An Indian curried meatball, made from meat or chicken, and fried.

Kosher : Food that is selected and prepared to Orthodox Jewish Law, including the traditional slaughtering ritual. Only the flesh of animals that 'chew cud' and have cloven hooves is permissible, and fish must have fins and scales. No birds of prey or scavengers are permitted in a Kosher diet.

Kringles : Rich short cakes.

Kromeskie : A Russian rissole made from rolled bacon, filled with minced meat, battered and deep-fried.

Krona Pepper : A variety of mild red pepper.

Kuban : A form of fermented milk.

Kugelhopf : Sweetened yeast cake containing dried fruit, and baked in a fluted tin.

Kuichai : A peppery version of a spring onion.

Kumara (Nz.) : See Sweet Potato.

Kumiss : A form of fermented milk.

Kümmel : A liqueur made from caraway seeds, fennel and orris root.

Kumquat : A very small, oval, orange-like citrus fruit, with bright orange-yellow, sweet-tasting, edible skin and juicy, slightly bitter flesh. May be eaten fresh with the skin, or used to make marmalade, or preserved in sugar syrup.

Kurrat : A vegetable almost identical to leeks.

Kuskus : Poppy seed, used in many subtle Eastern dishes.

Kuzo (Jap.) : A thickening agent made from the boiled and mashed roots of a Japanese vine, and used in the same way as arrowroot or cornflour, but is far superior as it contains protein. Can also be used as a glaze for desserts and puddings.

Kvass : A Russian mild beer-like drink made from rye flour.

Lablab Bean (Ind.) : (Bonavist, Callab or Hyacinth Bean). A legume of Asian origin, where it has the same uses as split pulses, though the raw beans can cause poisoning. They can be white, reddish, black or mottled, according to variety.

Lace : To add a small amount, or dash, of spirits, wine or strong flavouring to either a beverage or food preparation, either before, during or after cooking.

Lache : Small, delicate seafish, cooked as smelt.

Lactein Bread : (Milkloaf). A loaf to which milk or skimmed milk powder has been added during preparation.

Lactic Acid : The acid produced by the fermentation of milk sugar, and responsible for the flavour of sour milk and for example, the precipitation of the cassein curd into cottage cheese.

Lacto Ovo Vegetarian : The most common form of vegetarianism, which allows milk, eggs and all dairy products.

Lacto Vegetarian : As Lacto-ovo, but eggs are omitted.

Lactose : Milk sugar which constitutes about 5% of natural milk.

Lady's Fingers : See Okra. Also a short variety of banana.

Lady's Smock : See Cardamine.

Lagopus : A partridge with slightly bitter meat, that is prepared and cooked as grouse.

Lamb : The name and the meat of sheep that are younger than 12-14 months old, spring lamb should be younger than 6 months. It should have pale pink flesh with a fair amount of fat. The prime cuts being the legs and loins.

Lamballe : A term used to describe meat broth or soup.

Lamb's Lettuce : See Corn Salad.

Lamprey : Similar in appearance to and cooked as eel.

Lancashire Cheese : One of the best cheeses for cooking because of its high fat content. It has a crumbly texture and an off-white colour, and spreads very easily. Ideal for Welsh Rabbit (rarebit), or grated and added to soups or grilled dishes before cooking.

Land Cress : (American Cress). A variety of watercress that is rich in vitamins, and peppery-flavoured. A good substitute for watercress, and can also be cooked like spinach.

Langouste (Fr.) : A member of the Lobster family. Also see Crayfish.

Langoustine : See Dublin Bay Prawns.

Langres Cheese : A semi-hard or creamy cheese normally sold in slices.

Langue de Chat (Fr.) : Flat, finger-shaped crisp biscuit served with cold desserts. Literally means 'cats tongues'.

Laos (Sea) : A very, very delicate spice, sold in powder form and made from the root of the *Greater Galangal*. See Galangal.

Lapereau (Fr.) : A hare.

Lapin (Fr.) : A rabbit.

Larch Gum : A thickening agent or stabiliser, which is a good substitute for gum arabic.

Lard: Natural or refined fat, best made from the fat surrounding the stomach and kidney of pigs. Can be made from sheep and cattle, but it is not such a good quality. Pig lard is considered to be the best fat for pastry making.

Lardine : See Margarine.

Larding : Threading the lardoons through lean meat, using a special 'larding' needle, which prevents the meat becoming dry during roasting, or long slow cooking. See also Barding.

Lardoons : Narrow strips of fat in various lengths and thickness, used for larding.

Lard Substitute : Vegetable shortenings made from mixtures of partially hardened vegetable fats.

Lasagne (It.) : Wide ribbon noodles, sometimes coloured green and flavoured with spinach. Mainly used in baked dishes.

Latex : The milky sap of some plants which is used as normal cows' milk.

Lava : Edible seaweed. Lava bread is made by boiling lava in salted water, mincing, and mixing with oatmeal, and then baking as a normal flour loaf.

Lavaret : Freshwater fish of the Salmon family, and cooked as trout.

Laver Sauce : A sauce made with varieties of fine smooth seaweed.

Lax /Lox : Scandinavian for salmon, or American for smoked salmon.

Laxative : A purgative or substance accelerates the passing of food through the intestines, such as castor oil, senna or the vegetable rhubarb.

Leaf Beet : See Swiss Chard.

Leaven : A substance, such as barm, yeast, gluten or baking powder, which causes dough or batter to rise.

Leben : A type of fermented milk produced by boiling vigorously for about 10 minutes and then discarding the water. If eaten raw, or under-cooked, it can cause vomiting or diarrhoea.

Leeks : A vegetable that is a member of the *Liliaceae* or onion family, with the same flavour, but milder. Ideal for adding to stews and casseroles.

Left-Overs : A dish concocted from the remains of a previous meal, or where large amounts of meat are roasted, with the intention of providing cold meat dishes for another meal.

Legumes (Fr.) : Vegetables or plants with seed pods, such as peas, beans and lentils. In general, the dried seeds are known as Pulses, and the green legumes as Beans or Peas, depending on the type.

Legumin : A substance found in pulses, that when combined with chalk found in hard water, makes it difficult to cook them satisfactorily.

Leicester Cheese : A mild cheese with a flaky texture. Ideal for cooking, but dries out very quickly. A more compressed variety known as Red Leicester because of the orange-red colour of the rind is also available.

Lemon : The most versatile and widely used citrus fruit, except that it is too sour to be eaten raw. However, the zest or juice will add a nice tang to dishes such as fish, soups, savouries, curries and certain desserts, cakes, jams and pickles. Thin slices of lemon make a colourful, fresh garnish to many a display. The ascorbic acid in lemon juice will prevent oxidisation and discoloration of many fruits when prepared, like avocados, apples and bananas.

Lemonade : A drink made from lemon juice, sugar and soda water.

Lemon Balm : See Melissa.

Lemon Curd : A cooked mixture of sugar, butter, eggs and lemons, used as a dessert, pie filling or preserve.

Lemon Grass : A species of *Citronella* whose slender shoots possess the flavour and scent of lemon, due to the presence of citric oils. It is available dried, or powdered which is also known as Sereh powder.

Lemon Oil : The oil obtained from the peel of the fruit.

Lemon Sole : Variety of dab, but resembles a sole, but is less tasty. Cook as sole.

Lemon Thyme : A variety of thyme, that is less pungent than the main herb, and has a citrus flavour, which makes it ideal for custards.

Lentils : Seeds or pulses of a legume, normally dried and either green or orange-red which are soaked and used in soups, stews and purees. Although high in nutritional value, they lack some essential amino acids, and so are not a complete protein.

Lettuce : A very popular green salad vegetable of which there are four main types, namely cos, butterhead, crisphead and loose-leaf, each of which has its own special uses. See individual headings for details.

Leveret : A young hare, normally about 6-7 lbs. Can be recognised by its small sharp white teeth, smooth fur, and hidden claws. Hang for about one week. May be roasted whole to serve 4-6 persons.

Levroux Cheese (Fr.) : See Valencay.

Levulose : The sugar found in fruits.

Levure : A firm paste used to seal the lids of casseroles or cooking dishes to prevent the loss of any flavours by escaping steam.

Liaison : A thickener for soups and sauces, such as flour, cornflour, cornstarch, arrowroot or egg yolk.

Lichia : Similar to, and cooked as tuna.

Lift : To continuously turn over a mixture of dry ingredients by raising from the bottom to ensure a thorough blend of all the ingredients.

Lighten : A culinary term for reducing the consistency of a mixture by adding eggs or liquids.

Lights : A butchers term for the lungs from an animal carcass, and sold as offal.

Lima Beans : (Cape Peas). Similar to flagelot, and the size of broad beans. See Broad Beans.

Limandelle : Flat fish which is pale yellow one side, and white the other. Cook as plaice or brill.

Limburger Cheese : A soft cheese with a very strong smell and a spicy taste. It is made from whole cow's milk. The rind is brown and shiny, and the cheese inside is a bright yellow, with a few holes.

Lime : A citrus fruit similar to, but smaller than lemons, with a bright green colour and its own distinctive flavour. Can be used as a substitute for lemon in most cases, but it is a marvellous fruit in its own right.

Limpets : See Patella.

Line : To place shaped pieces of greaseproof paper or aluminium foil to the bottom of baking tins, or to cover the bases of pie dishes or pudding basins with dough.

Ling : The largest of the Cod family, with a similar textured and flavoured white flesh. An excellent substitute in all cod recipes. Available dried and salted.

Linguine (It.) : Flat ribbon-like spaghetti, often served with fish dishes.

Linseed : The tiny brown seeds of the *Flax* plant, used mainly in the production of linseed oil. Their smooth nutty flavour makes them a tasty and crunchy addition to freshly baked bread.

Liqueur : A flavoured alcoholic drink made from spirits, herbs and syrups.

Liquorice : The root of a small perennial legume, it can be bought as a dried root or as a powder. It is used in soft drinks, ice cream, candy, desserts, cakes and confectionary.

Litchi : See Lychee.

Livarot Cheese : A soft yellow cheese with a dark reddish-brown rind, made from skimmed milk. It has a strong flavour, and more pungent than Camembert.

Live Foods : Foods that have been allowed to ferment during their preparation or cooking process, such as bread, wine and yoghurt.

Liver : A part of offal that is an excellent source of minerals and vitamins, which is very much underestimated in its nutritional value, and like most offal, is easily digestible. See varieties such as calf, lamb, pig and ox for descriptions and uses. Animal liver is high in vitamins A,B and D, and fish liver high in vitamins A and D.

Loaves : Commonly known as Bread. Also a name for savoury mousse.

Lobster : A crustacean of which there are many varieties, which is basically slaty dark blue when alive or raw, turning to a pinky red or scarlet when cooked. It has a succulent, rich flavour, and is excellent either hot with a creamy sauce, or cold with salad and lemon wedges. The male lobster is brighter in colour, and smaller than the female, but has larger claws. The female has a broader tail and more tender flesh, and also contains the coral, spawn or eggs, which is used for lobster butter. When buying, choose one that feels heavy for its size, and the tail should spring back after straightening. Avoid white shells on the back, as this is a sign of old age. See also Crayfish.

Locksoy (Chin.) : Fine-drawn Chinese macaroni.

Locust Bean : See Carob Bean.

Loganberry : A tangy, juicy fruit, that has the shape of a blackberry, but elongated, and the colour of a raspberry, and are seedless. High in vitamin C.

Loin : The front part of a hindquarter of meat with the flank removed.

Longan : A pulpy fruit similar to lychee.

Longe (Fr.) : Top part of a loin, with particular reference to veal.

Long Grain Rice : See Patna and Basmati rice.

Long Potato : An alternative name for Sweet Potato.

Loose-Leaf Lettuce : A variety of lettuce that does not produce a heart. The leaves are curled, and picked like spinach - a few at a time without cutting the whole plant.

Loquats : (Japanese Medlars). A stone fruit, similar to an elongated plum, with a smooth, golden-yellow, orange or red-brown skin. The juicy cream-coloured flesh is slightly tart. Choose firm fruit.

Losange : Any food that is cut or formed into diamond shape moulds for garnishing.

Lotte : A rather tasteless white-fleshed fresh water fish, similar to and prepared as whiting.

Lotus Leaves (Chin.) : The leaves of the water-lily plant, usually dried and used for wrapping foods prior to cooking. Very fragrant, but require soaking before use.

Lotus Seeds (Chin.) : Seeds from the water-lily plant. Used in either meat or dessert dishes. Can be substituted by raw unsalted peanuts.

Lotus Roots (Chin.) : The roots of the water-lily, are a white sausage-shape which have a crunchy texture, and are sliced, and used as a vegetable. Sold either dried or canned. Can be substituted by pineapple.

Lovage : A herb of the *Angelica* family, whose leaves and ribs are eaten like celery.

Lox : See Lax.

Lukewarm : Approximately blood temperature i.e. 37° C (98.4° F).

Lumpy : Applies to dough that is not thoroughly mixed or smooth, and having a rough consistency.

Lute : A term used to describe the preparation of joints by sealing them with a dough of flour and water to retain the juices during cooking.

Lychees (Chin.) : (Litchi). A stone fruit, the size of a large cherry, with a hard, scaly skin, turning through pink to brown. The white pulpy flesh is firm and juicy, but slippery. Avoid fruits with a dry, shrivelled skin. Available fresh or canned.

Lyonnaise (Fr.) : In the Lyons style; usually with an abundance of onions, as in Lyonnaise sauce.

ℳ

Macadamia Nut (Austr.) : (Queensland Nut). Native to Australia. They are pale yellow, the same size as chestnuts, and are usually only available shelled and roasted. Used as a cocktail party nibble or in confectionary. Can also be puréed as required.

Macaroni /Maccheroni (It.) : A nourishing, medium-sized, thickish, tubular-shaped pasta which can vary in length and shape. See also Alimentary Paste and Spaghetti.

Macaroons : A round, dry almond flavoured, slightly chewy biscuit. See also Ratafia.

Maccaroncelli (It.) : (Favanti, Fovantini). Probably the largest of the Italian tubular-shaped pastas. See also Alimentary Paste.

Mace : It is part of the nutmeg, a fruit that looks like an apricot and grows on tall tropical trees. When ripe, the fruit splits to reveal the bright scarlet aril surrounding the shell of the seed; the dried aril is mace, and the kernel is nutmeg. Mace has a similar to the nutmeg but more delicate, and is sometimes used in meat or fish curries.

Macedoine (Fr.) : Mixture of fruit or vegetables, diced or cut into even-shaped pieces, and used as a garnish, or a mixture of flavoured fruit set in jelly.

Macerate : To soften food, or certain ingredients by soaking in liquid.

Macon : Bacon made from mutton.

Mackerel : An excellent and economical salt-water fish, rich in oil and vitamins. Ideal for grilling, frying, baking, or sousing. Can be purchased smoked, and served with salad and a fruity sauce. Must be used on the day of purchase, as it deteriorates quickly. The skin should be shiny and the flesh quite firm and stiff. See also Saurel.

Madagascar Bean : See Butter Bean.

Madeira : A rich dark sweet wine often used in food preparation. Also, a type of plain cake.

Madras : A common name used to describe fairly hot Indian curry dishes.

Madrilène : Generally refers to cold, clear soups flavoured with tomato juice.

Magma : A mixture of sugar syrup and sugar crystals produced during sugar refining.

Magnesium : An essential dietary substance, that is present in all chlorophyll, and therefore plentiful in all green plant foods. Necessary for maintaining muscle and nervous systems.

Magnesium Sulphate : See Epsom Salts.

Magnum : The name for a bottle, usually of champagne, which measures 1.5 litres.

Maintenon : Used to describe any preparation of fish or meat that is cooked in a paper case.

Maize : (Indian Corn). The grain of *Zea Mays.* There are a number of varieties used for different purposes. Flint corn and dent corn are used for flour. See also Sweetcorn and Popcorn.

Maize Flour : Highly refined and very finely ground maize, from which all germ and bran has been removed.

Maize Rice : (Mealie Rice). Finely cut maize with the germ and bran only partly removed.

Malaga : A popular sweet red or white wine, that is regularly used in cooking.

Maldive Fish : Dried tuna from the Maldive Islands, sold in packets, broken into small chips which need to be pulverised further before use. Can be an alternative to Dried Shrimp Paste.

Mallard : The largest wild duck, with lean, dry flesh, and is sufficient for 2-3 persons. Hang for one day only. Best served roasted.

Malpighia : See West Indian Cherry.

Malta Orange : See Blood Orange.

Malted Milk : A preparation of milk and malt extract. Available either evaporated or dry.

Malt Extract : The soluble part - mainly maltose, of malted grain (usually barley, but can be wheat), which is extracted by malting. Normally sold in a concentrated solution, jars, or in powder form. Used in producing homemade beers, hot or cold milk drinks, and for making special breads (malt loaf).

Malt Flour : Germinated barley or wheat, dried and ground. Add to wheat flour for making malt loaf.

Malting : A process of extracting maltose and dextrins by the use of hot water, from barley or wheat which has been allowed to sprout, when the starch is hydrolysed into maltose and dextrins.

Malt Loaf : A rich brown bread, which includes malt extract and raisins.

Maltose : Malt Sugar.

Malt Sugar : Used, mixed with soya sauce to give colour and crispness to meat or poultry skins when cooking. Can be substituted by brown sugar, with a little vinegar added.

Malt Vinegar : A type of vinegar made from malt, which is normally used for pickling and certain dressings rather than cooking, when varieties of cider or wine vinegar are preferred.

Manatee (W.I.) : See Sea-Cow.

Manche : The projecting bone of a meat cutlet.

Manchette : Paper frill used to cover the protruding bones of cutlets or joints. See also Papilotte.

Mandarin : A type of dessert orange, which is round, but flattened in shape, with loose oily bright orange skin, lightish flesh, and numerous pips, similar to tangerine.

Mandoline : A vegetable slicer with an adjustable blade.

Mange Tout : (Chinese, Snow, Sugar, and Eat-all Peas). A small fresh pea which is normally cooked and eaten in its pod.

Mango : Available in various shapes and sizes, and ranging in colour from green to yellowish-brown, but always have an orange-coloured flesh surrounding a central stone, and tasting slightly like peaches but more pungent. May be eaten raw, or as an ingredient in jams and chutneys. Can be bought fresh or canned. Also see Dried Mango.

Mango Powder : See Amchoor.

Mangosteen (Ind.) : A fruit the size of an orange, with thin purple rind and sweet white pulp in segments, as citrus fruit.

Manioc : See Cassava.

Manna : Dried escudate from the *Manna Ash* tree. Now used as a mild laxative.

Maple Syrup : The sap of certain *Maple* trees, evaporated into either syrup or sugar.

Maraschino : A dark red cherry, used mainly for producing maraschino liqueur, or decorating cakes and desserts.

Marbled : A term used to describe fine quality meat that is flecked with small pieces of fat.

Margarine : A butter substitute emulsion, made from animal or vegetable fat, or a mixture of both, dependant on the variety. It is available in solid form, which contains a higher percentage of saturated fat, or in soft form, which contains a higher percentage of water and is known as Unsaturated Margarine. It may be used for spreading, baking and frying, but is no substitute for butter regarding flavour.

Marinade : Blend of olive oil, wine or vinegar, lemon juice, herbs and spices. Used to tenderise and flavour meat, game or fish.

Marinate : The verb to steep in marinade.

Marinière (Fr.) : Describes mussels cooked in white wine and herbs, and served in their shells, or fish cooked in white wine and garnished with mussels.

Marjoram : A herb that must not be confused with Sweet or Wild Marjoram or Oregano, as they are a different species of plant. Its flavour is in fact, rather like thyme but sweeter and more scented. The leaves are used fresh or dried, chopped, crushed or powdered, in soups, stuffings, quiches, pies, omelettes, potato dishes and bouquet garnis. The delicate flavour is destroyed by cooking and should only be added just before completion of cooking. See also knotted marjoram.

Marmalade : Originally, a jam made from marmelo or quince, but now refers to a jam made from any citrus fruit, like orange, lemon, and grapefruit.

Marmelo : See Quince.

Marmite : A yeast extract, which is very high in proteins and vitamin B. It is used to flavour stocks, or can be spread on bread and eaten as a sandwich or aperitif. Marmite flavoured twiglets or thin biscuits are also available, which are pleasant when eaten with cheese or salad vegetables.

Marmite (Fr.) : An earthenware or metal stockpot, with a sealing lid used for the slow cooking of stews and casseroles. Also, a cooking term for stock.

Maroilles Cheese : A square, semi-hard, slightly salted yellow cheese with a reddish-brown rind, and a strong flavour and smell.

Marquise : Variety of soft, sweet pear.

Marrow : A vegetable which is a member of the Gourd family, which includes courgettes, chayotes, pumpkins and zucchini. They generally have a rather bland, watery taste and are best when mixed with other vegetables, either baked, stuffed, steamed or sauteed.

Marrow Bones : See Bone-Marrow.

Marrowfat Peas : A term used to describe the varieties of Wrinkled Garden Peas.

Marsala : A sweet Italian wine drunk as an aperitif, or used in cooking.

Marshmallow : Soft sweetmeat made from an aereated mixture of gelatin or albumin, and sugar or starch syrup. It has less glucose and more water than nougat, hence the softness.

Marzipan : (Almond Paste). A sweetmeat or cake decoration consisting 25% Almond Paste, and 75% Sugar.

Mascapone : Soft Italian cheese. Essential ingredient of Tiram su.

Mashing : In beer making, it is the process of heating malted barley, to help malting and fermenting.

Mash Tun : Vessel used in brewing, when mashing.

Mask : To cover food with an appropriate sauce, just before serving.

Mast : A type of Iranian fermented milk.

Matcha (Jap.) : Powdered green tea.

Maté : A herbal tea made from dried leaves of the *Ilex* tree.

Matelote (Fr.) : In the sailor's style; e.g. fish stew made with wine or cider.

Matoke : Steam-cooked green banana.

Matsutake (Jap.) : A Japanese type of mushroom.

Matzoh Meal : Made by grinding Matzohs (Jewish unleavened crispbreads made of wheatflour and water). It can be medium or fine, and is used mainly in Jewish cookery in Passover cakes and to thicken soups.

Mawseed : See Poppyseed.

Mayonnaise : A thick sauce made from egg yolks, oil and vinegar. Other ingredients such as mustard and garlic can be added.

Mazarines : Small moulds of fish, meat or game forcemeats, used as garnishes or entrées.

Mazun : Type of Armenian fermented milk.

Mead : An ancient alcoholic drink, made from herbs and fermented honey.

Meat : Generally refers to the muscle tissue of animals or birds. Non-muscle meat such as liver, heart or kidney is known as Offal or Organ Meat.

Meatballs : Balls of forcemeat boiled in salted water.

Meat Bar : A form of pemmican made from dehydrated cooked meat and fat.

Méchoui (Arabic) : A specialised Arab dish of slowly roasted meat, which must be constantly basted with melted butter, and evenly cooked throughout the joint, well roasted and crackling.

Medallions (Fr.) : Small circular or oval cuts of meat, fish or pâté.

Medlar : A very tart fruit which must be perfectly ripe before eating.

Megrim : A flat fish, rather dry and lacking in flavour. Should be served with a tangy or cheesy sauce.

Melangolo (It.) : See Bitter Orange.

Melba sauce : A sweet dessert sauce, made from peach, strawberry or raspberry purée.

Melba Toast : Thinly sliced white bread, with the crusts removed, cut diagonally, and then baked until crisp, and served with hors-d'oeuvres.

Melissa : (Lemon Balm). The light green leaves that smell of lemon, and used as a flavouring.

Mellorine : American for non butter-fat ice-cream.

Melon : A large juicy fruit, which is a member of the Gourd family. There are many varieties, all having a sweet, delicate flavour, often served in segments as a starter, but are a good addition to sweet and savoury salads, preserves, ice creams, sorbets and desserts. A ripe melon should yield slightly when pressed around the stem end.

Common varieties include cantaloupe, casaba, honeydew, ogen and water melons.

Melon Seeds : Used to flavour desserts.

Menu: A general term used to describe the bill of fare or courses available in a restaurant.

Mercury : See Good King Henry.

Merga : An Arabic sauce made with the juices of meat, and served with couscous.

Meringue (Fr.) : Whisked egg white blended with sugar, which is spooned or piped on top of sweet pies or into small shapes and baked crisp at very low temperature.

Mérou : Tasteless Mediterranean fish, cooked as tuna.

Meshimono (Jap.) : Rice combined with various other ingredients.

Mesocarp : See Albedo.

Methi (Ind.) : See Fenugreek.

Meunière (Fr.) : In the style of a miller's wife; e.g. fish cooked in butter, seasoned and sprinkled with parsley and lemon juice.

Meux Mustard (Fr.) : A grainy French mustard made from whole crushed mustard seeds. Can be substituted by most other wholegrain mustards.

Mexican Sage : See Oregano.

Middlings : The coarse remains of ground flour after it has been sieved or sifted.

Mignonette Pepper : Coarsely ground pepper.

Milanese (It.) : In the Milan style; escalopes coated in egg, breadcrumbs, seasoning and parmesan cheese, and fried in butter.

Milk : A nutritious liquid, which is the secretion of the mammary gland of animals, and is a complete protein food and high in calcium. Available in many forms including dried powder, and has many by-products such as cream, cheese and yoghurt.

Milk Loaf : See Lactein Bread.

Millet : (Teff). A small yellow grain with a pleasant nutty flavour, and high in fibre content, which can be used as a substitute for rice, but is more often used ground or flaked, and made into porridge or unleavened bread, due to its low level of gluten.

Milling : A manual process including grinding, for making flour from grain, or just 'cracking' the grain for flakes, or making white rice from brown rice.

Milt : Soft Roe of male fish.

Mimolette Cheese (Fr.) : A round orange cheese with grey rind. Similar to a hard dry cheddar.

Mincemeat (Eng.) : A mixture of marinated suet and dried fruits, used to fill tarts or small pies, (mince pies). The basic mixture can also include minced beef in some recipes.

Mincing : Chopping or cutting into small pieces, usually done with a hand mincer machine.

Mineola Fruit : See Tangelo.

Minerals : Soluble salts in food of which there are approximately 20 that are essential for our well being, of which 6 are needed in reasonably large quantities, these being:- sodium, chloride, potassium, calcium, phosphorous and magnesium.

Minestra (It.) : Describes thick Italian soup.

Minestrone (It.) : A thick savoury soup, which always includes pasta or rice as an ingredient.

Minnow : Small freshwater fish. Prepare and cook as, or substitute for Gudgeon.

Mint : A fresh tasting herb, with many varieties, of which spearmint and applemint are most important from the cook's point of view. Used mainly in lamb dishes, and as a garnish to salads and vegetables. It also forms the basis of mint sauce and mint jelly. Although best as fresh leaves, it is also useful in a dried form.

Minute : A term used to describe dishes which are cooked very quickly, and generally refers to under-done steaks.

Mirabelle (Fr.) : Small yellow plum, used as tart filling. Or a liqueur made from this fruit.

Mirepoix (Fr.) : A mixture of finely diced vegetables and ham or bacon which, when fried in butter, is used as a base for brown sauces and stews, or as a bed for braising meat.

Mirin (Jap.) : Sweet rice wine used for cooking only. Can be substituted by sweet sherry.

Mirliton : See Chayote.

Miso Paste : A naturally fermented paste made from soybeans and grains. Tastes very salty but is very high in protein. Used to flavour soups, sauces, dips etc. Can be either red (Aka Miso), or white (Shiro Miso).

Misoshiru (Jap.) : Thick, potage-type soup.

Mix : To gently combine ingredients together in a bowl or saucepan.

Mixed Grill : A grilled dish of various food items, which normally include lamb chops, sausages, kidneys, liver, bacon, tomatoes and mushrooms.

Mixed Herbs : A mixture of mild-sweet herbs, used extensively in continental cooking.

Mocca/ Mocha/ Moka : High quality coffee served after dinner, sometimes blended with various chocolate flavours.

Mochi (Jap.) : Rice cake.

Mochiko (Jap.) : Flour made from glutinous rice.

Moistening : The actual liquid ingredient, or the process of adding the liquid to a preparation, to assist the cooking process.

Molasses : A very sweet and strongly-flavoured by-product of sugar, often used in cakes and desserts.

Molbo Cheese : A mild-flavoured pale yellow Danish cheese with a red rind, which has a slightly acid after-taste. Close-textured with a few holes.

Mollusc : A group of shellfish, including mussels, oysters and scallops, which mainly have hinged shells.

Monkey Bread : See Baobab.

Monkey Nut : See Peanut.

Monkfish : A deliciously flavoured, firm and textured fish, that makes an excellent substitute for scampi, and at a much lower price.

Monosodium Glutamate : See M.S.G.

Mooli : A mild tasting Japanese radish that can be grated, used as a garnish, pickled, or cooked like turnip.

Moorhen : See Coot.

Moose : (Elk). The largest member of the deer family. Prepare and cook as deer.

Moray : Similar to, and cooked as eel.

Morel : Small, black pointed fungus, cooked as cèpes.

Morello Cherry : Dark red /black skinned cherry with firm, sweet red flesh.

Mornay : A cheese sauce used to coat fish, egg or vegetable dishes.

Mortar : A heavy stone deep round bowl used with a pestle to pound and grind whole spices.

Morven Cheese : A mild Scottish cheese made in small squares, and has a full flavour and texture, similar to Dutch Gouda. Sometimes flavoured with caraway seeds.

Mossberry : See Cranberry.

Mouiller : To add a small amount of liquid to a meat preparation during the cooking process.

Mouler (Fr.) : To grind into a puree, or dry food into a powder.

Moules (Fr.) : French word for Mussels.

Moussache : Manioc flour used to produce tapioca.

Moussaka : Greek dish of minced lamb, aubergines and tomatoes, which is topped with cheese sauce.

Mousse : Light sweet, or savoury cold dish made with cream, whipped egg, white wine and gelatine.

Moyashi (Jap.) : See Bean Sprout.

Mozzarella Cheese (It.) : An Italian soft curd cheese that is moulded into a flask, egg or ball shape and tied with raffia. It has slightly sour taste and a fairly thick rind. Used extensively in making pizza fillings.

M.S.G. : A shortened version of monosodium glutimate, which is a powder used sparingly to enhance the flavour of dishes, and a common ingredient in Chinese recipes.

Muesli (Sw.) : Dish of raw rolled oats, coarsely grated apple, nuts and dried fruit, served with cream or milk.

Muffins : Thick, well-aerated dough cakes cooked on a griddle or hotplate. Less tough than crumpets.

Mulberry : Similar to blackberry. Used to make jams or jellies.

Mull : To heat and also spice or flavour ale and wine.

Mullet (Grey) : Well flavoured estuary fish, with coarse, oily, firm flesh. Ideal for baking. Must be descaled before cooking.

Mullet (Red) : A very tasty red-skinned saltwater fish normally grilled or baked whole. Not related to grey mullet. The liver is considered to be a delicacy.

Mulligatawny : Highly spiced and curried thick broth which includes either pasta or rice.

Mung Beans : Small olive green beans, available whole, split and skinless. Often used in stews, curries, or as a vegetable in salads. Best known as being used for growing bean sprouts, which can be eaten raw or made into pea-starch noodles or cellophane.

Murlins : See Alaria.

Muscade : See Nutmeg.

Muscatel : Dried, large, seedy grapes, mainly grown in Spain. Normally pressed flat. Also a sweet wine made from the same grape.

Mushimono (Jap.) : Steamed foods.

Mushrooms : A favourite fungi, of which the most common types are the button - small roundish shaped, and the field variety which are much larger and flatter. May be grilled, fried or added to dishes such as soups and pizzas, or eaten raw as an addition to salads. See also Parasol Mushrooms.

Mussel : A very cheap, but tasty Mollusc, whose juices add a distinctive flavour to many seafood, soup and sauce dishes. Before cooking, discard any with broken shells or do not close when tapped. After cooking, any which float should be thrown away.

Must : The juice or liquid produced from pressed fruit or vegetables before fermentation begins.

Mustard : A condiment paste made from mustard seeds to which other different ingredients may or may not be added and for which there are numerous recipes, although it is normally purchased as a commercial product.

Mustard And Cress : Seedlings of sprouted cress and mustard used raw in salads and sandwiches, especially with eggs or cheese. Mild-flavoured Rape seed can be substituted for the rather peppery white Mustard.

Mustard Greens : See Chinese cabbage.

Mustard Seed : Sharp and pungent, either white, yellow or black, and used either whole or freshly ground.

Mutton : The meat of sheep more than one year old, which is generally darker and fatter than lamb or beef. The meat should be bright red, firm and close-grained. There should be a fair amount of firm, white fat around the meat.

Myrtle : An evergreen shrub whose fragrant leaves are used as bayleaves, and the berries are ground to produce a form of pepper.

Naan (Ind.) : A North Indian bread traditionally cooked in a tandoor oven. Made from unleavened dough, and oval in shape.

Naartje : A small seedless orange-like fruit, with loose bright orange skin, like tangerines. Available fresh, or as crystallised whole fruit.

Nabemono (Jap.) : Dishes cooked on an open fire, in a cauldron or saucepan.

Nage : Lobster, cooked in court bouillon.

Nam Pla : An Indonesian fish sauce made from fresh anchovies and salt.

Nappa (Chin.) : See Chinese Cabbage.

Napper : To cover a preparation with a thick layer of sauce, jam or jelly, and then garnished.

Narcissus : Edible bulbs prepared and cooked as Jerusalem artichokes.

Naruto (Jap.) : Steamed fish cake.

Naseberry Plum : See Sapodilla.

Nasturtium : See Indian Cress.

National Flour : See Wheatmeal.

Natives : A term used to describe oysters spawned and bred in purpose-built beds.

Natto (Jap.) : Fermented Soya Bean.

Navarin (Fr.) : A brown stew of lamb with onions, potatoes and /or vegetables.

Navel Orange : Thin smooth-skinned oranges which are distinguished by the raised embryo growth at one end. They have juicy flesh with few pips.

Navets (Fr.) : French name for turnips.

Navy Beans : See Haricot Beans.

Neapolitan (It.) : Ice creams and sweet cakes in layers of different colours and flavours.

Neat : An old name for ox tongue.

Neats Foot : Old name for Cow's Heel. Also oil obtained from knuckle bones of cattle, which is used for canning sardines. See Cows Heel.

Neck : The section of an animal between the head and shoulders. Suitable for stews and casseroles.

Nectar : A term used to describe any type of sweet drink. The Greek word meaning 'Drink of the Gods'.

Nectarine : (Brugnon). Smooth-skinned stone fruit that is a variety of peach, with a juicy sweet flesh. Does not keep.

Negi (Jap.) : Green onion.

Nelson : A dish of steak fillet placed between layers of sliced potato and onions, and cooked slowly in a casserole.

Nephrop : See Dublin Bay Prawns.

Nèroli : Oil extracted from orange blossom, and used in flavouring confectionary.

Nests (Chin.) : Washed and prepared nests of the salagne bird, used in Chinese cookery to hold other food preparations.

Niboshi (Jap.) : Dried young sardine.

Niçoise (Fr.): In the Nice style; e.g. with tomatoes, onion, garlic, anchovy and olives.

Nigella : Variety of plants whose seeds are used to produce a kind of pepper.

Nimono (Jap.) : Boiled food.

Nioigome : Perfumed rice.

Nip : A quarter bottle of wine or spirits.

Nira (Jap.) : Scallion or leek.

Nishime (Jap.) : Cooked vegetable dish.

Nisin : A natural antibiotic found in cheese. Used to prolong the storage life of milk products and canned fruit fish and vegetables.

Noggin : A measure of liquid equal to ¼ of an Imperial Pint.

Noisettes: Neatly trimmed and tied pieces of meat, normally beef or lamb, and approximately 1cm or 1/2 inch thick.

Nonat : Small delicate fish, normally deep-fried.

Non-Pareils : Silver beads made from sugar coated with foil, and used to decorate confectionary.

Noodles : A pasta made from flour, water and eggs, of which there are many varieties, dependant mainly on the type of flour used, namely:- wheat (the most common), rice, buckwheat, soya beans, arrowroot, and all manner of starchy substances.

Nori (Jap.) : Purple laver or seaweed that is pressed into paper-thin sheets, and usually toasted to bring out the flavour before using as a wrapper around rice, or as a garnish.

Normande, a la (Fr.) : In the Normandy style, e.g. cooked with cider and cream.

Normandy Pippins : See Biffins.

Norway Lobster : See Dublin Bay Prawns.

Nougat : Sweetmeat made from a mixture of gelatin or egg albumin, with sugar and starch syrup, which has been thoroughly aereated.

Nouilles (Fr.) : Noodles.

Nouvelle Cuisine (Fr.) : Highly artistic, beautifully presented cooking popularised in the eighties. Characterised by exceedingly small portions.

Noxipan : A marzipan made from hazelnuts in place of almonds.

Nubbing : Term used for 'topping and tailing' fruit. See also Snibbing.

Nutmeg : (Muscade) The kernel of the *Mace* plant, normally sold ground, but can be bought whole and grated as required for maximum flavour. Sweet and mildly spicy, it is used to flavour egg, cheese and quiche dishes, curries, meats, cakes, puddings and bakery products.

Nutrients : Essential dietary substances such as vitamins, minerals, amino acids and fats.

Nutro Biscuit : Made from 60% wheatflour and 40% peanut flour.

Nuts : Hard-shelled kernel or fruit of trees. High in fat and protein.

Oat Flakes : (Rolled Oats). Whole grains of oats, crushed by rollers and partially cooked.

Oat Flour : Ground oats with the bran removed.

Oat Groats : Whole husked oat grains or kernels. High in fibre and nutritional content, and used in oat cakes, haggis, granola bars, muesli products, rissoles and croquettes.

Oatmeal : (Ground Oats). Milled oat grains, after the husks have been removed, which comes in various forms of coarseness, generally used in broths and forms of porridge. Also an American term for Porridge.

Oats : A grain, used whole to make dishes such as porridge.

Oblade : Fish, similar to and cooked as bream.

Octopus : A cephalopod mollusc whose tentacles' hard flesh is beaten to soften prior to cooking.

Offal : (Abats, Organ Meat or Variety Meat). Edible internal organs of meat, poultry or game which are cut away when the carcass is dressed. Does not keep well, and is best used on day of purchase.

Ogen : A variety of melon.

Oil : Liquid fat, not soluble in water, produced from animals and vegetables, used in food preparation and cooking.

Oilseed : Seeds grown specifically for their oil, such as groundnut, sesame, soya and sunflower.

Oily Fish : Refers to species of fish where oil is present throughout the whole of its flesh. See White fish.

Oka : A rich tasty Canadian cheese. Also a small rough tuber normally boiled or puréed.

Okayu (Jap.) : Rice gruel.

Okra : (Lady's fingers, Bamies, Bamya, Gumbo and Ketmie). Can be bought fresh or canned, but preferably fresh. A good addition to certain spicy dishes, including curries, but is more often fried, steamed or sauteed, with onions and spices, and served separately as a side dish. The slightly slimy texture can be removed by salting.

Olives : The fruit of a Mediterranean evergreen tree. Either green (unripe), or black (ripe). Almost always sold pickled, whole, stoned or stuffed with red pepper or tomato puree. Used mainly as a finger food, but are also useful in salads, pizzas and cooked savoury dishes. The fresh fruits are kept by the growers for the production of olive oil.

Olive Oil : An oil produced from the pressings of the ripe (black) fruit, available in various grades of quality, depending on the number of previous pressings - the earlier the pressing, the better the quality. See Extra Virgin Oil, the most superior of olive oils. Used in various salad dressings, or as a cooking ingredient in many European and Eastern dishes.

Omelette : A versatile preparation of beaten eggs, seasoned and fried in a small amount of butter. The variations of cooking, and fillings are too numerous to mention in detail.

Onion : A plant of the *Liliaceae* family, and one of the most common vegetables, used in most countries and many varied recipes. Normally used fresh, chopped or sliced to release the flavour, and added raw to salads, or added to many dishes as an important ingredient. Can be bought chopped and dried for convenience. See also Shallots and Racambole.

Open Tart : A tart which has no pastry top.

Orach : (French Spinach). Green-leaved plant cooked as spinach.

Orange : A citrus fruit of which there are many dessert or sweet varieties, such as blood, jaffa and navel, and bitter varieties such as seville, which are used almost exclusively for making marmalade.

Orange Agaric : An orange-red mushroom with a pleasantly spicy flavour and smell and brittle flesh. Best used fresh, in sauces or soups. It is also good when pickled.

Oregano : (Mexican Sage). A strong flavoured herb, similar to marjoram, but more pungent. Used extensively in Italian meat and vegetable dishes. Although available fresh, it is most frequently used dried. An ideal ingredient for sausages and sausagemeat dishes.

Organic : Any substances of animal or vegetable origin.

Organ Meat : See Offal.

Organt : See Wild Marjoram.

Orientale : Term applied to fish, eggs, or vegetables, that are prepared and cooked with tomatoes, garlic and saffron.

Orly : Term applied to fillets of fish that are battered, then deep-fried and served with tomato sauce.

Ormer : See Abalone.

Orris : A root used in the production of kummel liqueur.

Ortanique : A hybrid citrus fruit, being a cross between a tangerine and an orange, and similar in size to a navel orange, but flattish in shape, very juicy, and would make a very good substitute for either.

Ortolan : Small bird, considered a delicacy. It is normally wrapped in vine leaves or bacon, then either cooked on a spit, or roasted in its own juices.

Oshibori (Jap.) : A damp and scented soft towel used to cleanse the hands during and after a meal.

Oshitashi (Jap.) : Greens boiled in soy sauce.

Osso Buco (It.) : Dish of braised marrow bones, prepared with tomato and wine.

Oursins : See Sea-urchins.

Ovenspring : A cooking term used to describe the sudden rise in volume of dough during the first 10-12 minutes if baking, due to the increased rate of fermentation and the expansion of trapped gases.

Ox : See Beef.

Ox-cheek : The flesh found on either side of an ox head.

Oxtail : Normally sold ready skinned and jointed. The fat should be a creamy-white and the lean meat a deep red. Ideal for braising or in a casserole, or as a basis for thick soups.

Ox-Tongue : See Tongue.

Oxymel : Syrup made from honey and vinegar.

Oyster : A slightly salty-tasting bi-valved mollusc. Usually eaten raw, but may be lightly cooked. Shells should be shut or close when tapped. Must be absolutely fresh, and opened only just before serving if raw.

Oyster Plant : See Salsify.

Oyster Sauce (Chin.) : A dark, thick, strong and salty sauce used sparingly to season Chinese cooking, or as a condiment on vegetables.

Pacific Prawn : Similar to Dublin Bay Prawn, but even larger, being some 120-150 mm. long.

Paella (Sp.) : Dish of saffron rice, chicken, shellfish and vegetables, which is named after the iron two-handled pan in which it is cooked.

Pain (Fr.) : French for Bread.

Pak-Choy : See Chinese Cabbage.

Palette knife : In culinary terms, a long, wide flexible smooth-edged instrument, used to spread icing, or other soft toppings over cakes and confectionary.

Palmae : A species of tree that includes the palms that produce dates and coconuts.

Palm Oil : Extraction from the pericarp or outer pulp of the palm nut. A major source of oil for cooking and making margarine.

Palm Sugar : (Gula Jawa, Gula Malaka). This dark strong-flavoured sugar is obtained from the sap of coconut palms and palmyrah palms. The sap is boiled down until it crystallises, and the resultant sugar is normally sold in round, flat cakes or thin blocks. Can be substituted by black sugar or refined dark brown sugar.

Palta : See Aguneate.

Panada : A thick sauce or paste made from flour or bread, fat and liquid such as milk or stock, which is used to bind ingredients together, such as croquettes or meatballs, or as a basis for souffles and choux pastry.

Panary Fermentation : Yeast fermentation of dough in breadmaking.

Pancakes : (Hotbreads). A dessert made from a thin cream-like batter heated in a greased pan.

Pancreas : The sweetbread or thymus gland of sheep or calf, which is considered a delicacy, and often grilled and eaten on toast.

Pandanus : (Screwpine, Rampe). The long, flat green leaves of the plant are either crushed or boiled to yield its distinctive flavour which is as popular in the East, as vanilla is in the West.

Pandoras : Sections of toast covered with a savoury mixture, then dipped in batter and deep-fried.

Panetière (Fr.) : Term applied to dishes where various meats, when cooked, are placed in hollow loaves and baked until brown.

Panettone (It.) : Cake-like bread with raisins, which is served at Christmas.

Panir (Ind.) : A simple curd cheese made from milk and natural yoghurt.

Pannequets : Pancakes spread with various sweet mixtures, then rolled or folded, glazed and then baked or grilled.

Panocha : A Persian sweetmeat.

Papaya : See Pawpaw.

Papillote : Paper frills used to decorate various dishes, particularly meat to hide the bone-ends. Also the name given to food that is wrapped in greaseproof paper to retain the juices, before baking or steaming.

Paprika (Hung.) : (Hungarian Pepper). Ground sweet red pepper, with an attractive red-orange colour.

Parasol Mushroom : Probably the largest edible mushroom available.

Paratha : A fancy chapati, layered with fat like making puff pastry.

Par-Boiling : Boiling for a short time to partially cook food, usually to preserve it or keep it moist, before completing cooking by another method.

Parchita : See Passion Fruit.

Parfait (Fr.) : Frozen dessert made of whipped cream and fruit purée garnished with nuts.

Paring : To peel or trim vegetables and fruit.

Parkin : A ginger cake made with oatmeal, treacle or syrup.

Parmentier (Fr.) : Applied to dishes containing potatoes as a main ingredient.

Parmesan Cheese (It.) : A hard, strong and fragrant Italian cheese, making it ideal for cooking, which is off-white inside its black rind. In grated form, it is used extensively in soups, vegetable and pasta dishes.

Parisienne, a la (Fr.) : Applies to garnishes that must always include small round balls of potato.

Parrot Fish : (Scarus). A fine-fleshed Mediterranean fish, bright red in colour. Used mainly in court-bouillon or fried.

Parsley : A mild fresh-flavoured herb used extensively in egg and cheese dishes, and as a garnish for many meat casserole or salad dishes. A very versatile herb. Available dried, but best to use fresh if possible.

Parsnip : A sweet-tasting fairly strong flavoured root vegetable, that can be either roasted as a potato, or boiled, or added to a stew or casserole.

Parson's Nose : The soft end portion of the rear end of a fowl.

Partridge : A game bird, of which there are two main varieties, the English (grey), which has the best flavour, and the slightly larger French partridge. Young birds have round-tipped feathers, yellow-brown pliable feet, and light-coloured plump flesh. Hang for about three days before roasting or grilling.

Passion Fruit : (Granadilla or Parchita). A knobbly-skinned purplish-brown fruit, with a sweet and juicy, strong tangy flavoured orange pulp, with small black edible seeds.

Pasta (It.) : Literally meaning 'dough', there are many different varieties, shapes, colours and sizes, but is actually sold in two main forms:- the factory made dried pasta made from flour and water, normally available in packets, and the home made fresh pasta made from flour and eggs. Although pasta should only be made from semolina flour milled from durum wheat, ordinary plain/all-purpose flour can be used quite successfully. See also Alimentary Paste.

Paste : (Pâté). A general term to describe bread and pastry doughs, or batters. In English culinary terms, this word also describes a fine mixture of herbs and meat, which is to spread on bread slices, or as Pâté.

Pasteurisation : Part sterilisation, usually of milk, which prolongs storage life for a limited period.

Pastina (It.) : A small variety of macarino used mainly in soups.

Pastry : Generally refers to the food item produced from cooking a paste or pastry dough.

Pasty : A circle of flaky pastry, filled with a savoury mixture, then folded over, in half, and baked. Eaten as a snack. See also Turnover.

Pâte : See Paste.

Pâté : A savoury preparation of finely minced and herbed meat or fish. Also applies to that preparation when encased in puff pastry and baked as a pie. Can be served hot or cold.

Patella : Univalve mollusc, eaten raw as oysters.

Patis : A spicy shrimp or fish sauce, available from Oriental stores.

Pâtisserie (Fr.) : Term applied to pastry dishes, that are generally baked in the oven. Also the name of a shop selling pastry items.

Patna Rice : A long-grain white rice, but not of the same quality as basmati rice.

Patties : Individual pies served hot from the oven and often eaten by hand as a snack.

Patty Tin : A moulded tin for baking a batch of small cakes.

Paunching : To remove the stomach and intestines of a rabbit or hare.

Paupiette (Fr.) : Thin slice of savoury meat filling, covered with a rasher of bacon and shallow-braised.

Pavé (Fr.) : Cold savoury mousse mixture set in a square mould coated with aspic jelly, or square sponge cake, filled with butter cream and coated with icing.

Pawpaw : (Papaya). A fruit that normally has a yellow skin with bright pink flesh containing tiny black seeds which have a peppery flavour, and should be removed before eating. The flesh is fairly sweet when ripe, and makes a good breakfast substitute for grapefruit. Choose fruit which feels slightly soft to the touch. Rich in vitamin A and C.

Pea : Available fresh, frozen, canned or dried. They can be boiled, steamed, puréed or added directly to soups, savoury dishes and casseroles. A very versatile vegetable. Fresh peas can be either cooked and eaten in their pods or removed from their pods before use, depending on the variety and age. See Mange-tout, Petits Pois, Garden, Green and Processed.

Dried peas must be soaked overnight before using. The term Pea is normally reserved for fresh green vegetable peas, and the dried varieties such as chick and pigeon peas are termed as Pulses.

Peach : A top fruit with sweet juicy flesh, a hard centre stone, and a hairy textured skin. Avoid any with split or bruised skins, or brown soft spots. Ideal eaten whole, or in a fruit salad.

Peanut : (Monkeynut, Earthnut, Groundnut). Available whole or shelled, and can be eaten plain or roasted. Used to make peanut butter or oil. Technically a legume rather than a nut.

Peanut Butter : A paste made from skinned, ground and roasted peanuts which has a strong flavour which may be added to some stews or casseroles, but should be used sparingly. It also makes a very good savoury snack when spread on bread or toast.

Pear : A top fruit, that like apples, is available either as a dessert or cooking fruit. They bruise easily, and should be handled with care. Ripe pears will yield when gently pressed at the stem. Common varieties of dessert pear are Conference, Dayenne du Comice and William.

Pearl Barley : A refined version of pot barley, and is therefore far less nutritious. It takes only 15 minutes to cook and is mainly used in soups and stews.

Pearled Hominy : Degermed hulled maize. See also Hominy.

Pearl Haricot : A small haricot used for making baked beans and cassoulet.

Pease Pudding : Purée of cooked, dried peas which is made into puddings, boiled and served with pork.

Pecan Nut : Similar in flavour and appearance to walnuts, but oilier. Their shells are a smooth shiny red and much easier to remove. Popular in the US, where they are used to make pecan pie.

Pecten : A species of bivalve mollusc, with rounded, deep-grooved shells, the most common of which is the scallop.

Pectin : Substance extracted from fruit (especially the pith), and vegetables. Used to set jellies and jams, and added to ice cream as an emulsifier.

Peel : The outer skin of fruit and vegetables, or the operation of removing it. See also Rind.

Pelagic Fish : Fish that swim near the surface, and are mostly oily types like herring and mackerel.

Pemmican : A cake of dried powdered meat and fat of a buffalo or deer.

Pepper : The common pepper, normally used at table, and not to be confused with sweet or red peppers, (pimentos), are the berries from the pepper vine plant. Available as whole green, black or white peppercorns, and as black or white ground pepper. The green corns or berries are picked and then sun-dried, which turns them black. The white peppercorns are simply green peppercorns which have been left to ripen fully. Green peppercorns have a fresh and pungent flavour, and are usually sold pickled in brine. Black and white peppers are similar in flavour, but the black is the more pungent of the two. A very versatile spice.

Pepper Cayenne : See Cayenne pepper.

Perch : (Aceline). A round freshwater fish with brightly coloured hard scales. Best when grilled whole. See bass.

Percolator : Two-part coffee pot which forces boiling water from the lower half, up through the coffee grains contained in the upper half, and then filtered through to the bottom half ready for drinking.

Perdrix (Fr.) : A term used to describe old partridge which are used mainly for making forcemeats and purées due to the tough meat.

Pericarp : In reference to cereal grain, it is the fibrous layers next to the outer husk, which are normally removed during milling. A major constituent of bran.

Periwinkle : See Winkle.

Perry : A word for fermented pear juice, as cider is to apple juice.

Persimmon : (Kaki, Sharon fruit, Date Plum). They look like large orange tomatoes, and have the same succulent flesh, with a slightly peachy flavour. They are very unpleasant when under-ripe, so wait until they are soft before eating. Best enjoyed on their own or in a fruit salad, but can be added to cakes or made into jams or chutneys.

Pestle : A fairly heavy, hard, rounded implement used to pound ingredients such as whole spices in conjunction with a mortar.

Pesto (It.) : Basil, olive oil and garlic paste used mainly in pasta dishes.

Peter's Cress: See Samphire.

Petit Fours (Fr.) : Tiny sponge cakes or biscuits, iced and decorated, or small fruits, e.g. grapes and cherries, coated in sugar glaze, or marzipan, coloured and shaped to resemble miniature fruits, or small biscuits.

Petit Pois (Fr.) : The finest variety of tiny young green peas, which are very tender and have a sweetish flavour. Similar varieties are Indian peas and Pigeon peas.

Petit Poussin (Fr.) : A baby chicken, 4-6 weeks old. Suitable for grilling or spit-roasting. Allow one per person.

Petit Suisse Cheese : A very creamy unsalted cheese, made from whole milk and extra cream. It has a faintly sour flavour, and often eaten with sugar. Sold wrapped, in small individual rolls.

Pe-Tsai : See Chinese Cabbage.

Pheasant : A game bird, where the cock or hen may be sold singly or as a brace. Young birds of both sexes should have pliable beaks and feet, and soft pointed feathers. A hen is considered the tastiest, and serves two to three.

Picarel : Small fish prepared as anchovy.

Piccalilli : Pickle made from vegetables, mustard, vinegar and various spices.

Pickerel : Young Pike.

Pickled Cabbage (Chin.) : Yellow-green in colour, and sold in jars or cans. Chop or slice, and add to steamed or stir-fried dishes to add a tangy flavour. Rinse before use to remove brine. Can be substituted by sauerkraut and salt.

Pickles : Preserved vegetables in a vinegar and spice solution.

Pickling : (Brining). Generally applied to beef or pork cured in a brine of water and 5-10% salt and saltpetre. See also Pickles.

Pickling Onion : A small silverskin variety of button onion, which is pickled in vinegar and spices, for use as cocktail onions.

Pickling Spice : A traditional blend of mild and hot spices used for pickling meats, herrings, mackerel, eggs, and vegetables such as beetroot and onions.

Picnic : An open air meal eaten during trips or excursions, normally consisting of cold fare.

Picnic Ham (U.S.) : See Foreleg of Ham.

Pie : A dish consisting of a pastry case with either sweet or savoury fillings, and covered with a layer of pastry (lid). See tart or flan.

Pièce de Résistance (Fr.) : A culinary term which refers to the chef's speciality dish with which he displays his best culinary skills. Also refers to the main course of a meal.

Pie Funnel : A funnel used to support a pastry lid.

Pig : See Pork.

Pigeon : (Squab). Normally refers to wood pigeon, which is a game bird, normally tough and best casseroled. Very young birds, with pink legs, downy feathers and plump breast, may be roasted or grilled. Hang for one day, and serve one bird per person.

Pigeon Pea : See Petit Pois.

Pigfish : See Triggerfish.

Pigs Fry : The interior elements of a pig.

Pigs Trotters : May be used instead of calf's foot for making jellied stock, and as a base for lentil soup, or adding to brawns.

Pike : A large, lean freshwater fish with a long body, and firm, white, coarse flesh, and needs soaking or boiling in court-bouillon before being baked or poached.

Pikelets : Dough cakes made from thinned-down Crumpet batter.

Pilaf/Pilau (Turk.) : A popular Near-Eastern dish of cooked rice mixed with spiced, cooked meat, chicken or fish. The rice grains are fried in ghee or oil before boiling.

Pilchard : A small saltwater fish, similar to herring, which deteriorate quickly. Normally sold tinned in spiced oil.

Pilot Fish : A tasty fish, similar to, and cooked as mackerel.

Pimento Berries: See Allspice.

Pimiento : Green, red or yellow pepper, of the *Capsicum* family, used raw in salads, or fresh garnish, or cooked with other vegetables such as onions and tomatoes to enhance a variety of Continental and Eastern dishes.

Pimpernel : A herb with the flavour of cucumber. Often used in soups and salads.

Pinch : In culinary terms, refers to the amount of powder that can be held lightly between the thumb and forefinger, approximately 2 grams.

Pineapple : Large oval fruit with hard, knobbly top skin, which varies from deep yellow to orange-brown. The firm flesh is sweet and juicy. Normally cut into chunks and added to a fruit salad, but can be cooked and added to various savoury dishes.

Pine Nut : (Indian nut). Small, soft nuts that can be eaten raw or roasted and salted like peanuts, and make a good alternative. When fresh, they may smell quite strongly of turpentine, which is a product of some *Pine* trees, but this fades during storage, and is why they are normally sold shelled.

Pine Seed : Kernels of pine cones which have a similar taste to almonds.

Pinion : The terminal segment of a bird's wing. See Giblets.

Pink Shrimps : This shrimp has a grey shell which turns rosy-pink when boiled. They are less tasty than brown shrimps, and usually sold cooked and unpeeled.

Pint : A standard Imperial measure, equal to 1/8 gallon.

Pintade (Fr.) : Guinea fowl.

Pintail : Variety of wild duck.

Pinto Beans : (Tepary or Frijole Beans). Speckled beans which normally come in various shades of pink and brown. Often used in Mexican dishes, soups, salads and pâtes.

Pipe : To force meringue icing, savoury butter, potato purée etc., through a forcing bag fitted with a nozzle, to decorate various dishes.

Pipérade : A fluffy purée of tomatoes, eggs and peppers.

Piping Bag : See Forcing Bag.

Pippin : A type of apple incorporating several popular species, such as cox's orange pippin.

Piquante (Fr.) : Used to describe a pleasantly sharp and appetising taste or aroma.

Piquer (Fr.) : To insert into meats or poultry a large julienne of fat, bacon, ham or truffle for example.

Piroghi /Pirozhki (Russ.) : Two Russian words to describe large and small pies.

Pissalat : A condiment made from sieved pickled herring preserved in spiced urine.

Pistachio Nut : Available whole or shelled, they are a delicious green coloured nut, which is best when roasted and salted, or can be added to ice cream, halva, salads and stuffings, to enhance the flavour as well as the colour. They are sold in their natural coloured tan shells, or dyed red.

Pistole : Variety of plum, normally stoned and dried as prunes.

Pistou (It.) : Vegetable and vermicelli soup, combined with garlic and grilled tomatoes.

Pith : (Albedo). In citrus fruit, the white cellular lining to the rind covering the flesh.

Pitta Bread : Middle Eastern unlevened bread.

Pizza (It.) : Open-faced pie consisting of a rich yeast dough, topped with a variety of toppings, including tomatoes, mozzarella cheese, ham, tuna, anchovies and olives to name but a few.

Pizzaiola (It.) : Meat or chicken, cooked in red wine, tomato sauce and flavoured with garlic. Also refers to the chef who makes pizzas.

Plaice : Flat fish with soft white flesh suitable for poaching, grilling, or frying. Cook small fish whole on the bone and larger fish in fillets. Does not keep very well.

Plain / All-Purpose Flour : White wheatflour that is used for general cooking and baking. It may include certain additives such as emulsifiers, colourings, flavourings, preservatives and anti-oxidants to prolong shelf life.

Plantain : A fruit identical in looks to a banana, but normally much larger, and not as sweet. It must however be cooked before eating and like a cooking apple cannot be eaten raw. Can be boiled and mashed, or sliced and fried.

Plastron : Soft, lower part of a turtle shell, used mainly in turtle soup.

Plat du Jour (Fr.) : Dish of the day.

Platter : A large oval serving plate.

Plover : A game wading bird, prepared and cooked as woodcock.

Pluck : A butchers term for a mixture of offal, or to remove the feathers from a bird.

Plum : This fruit falls into two main categories, dessert and cooking, although there are many varieties of each. Choose firm, plump fruit that yields evenly to gentle pressure without being oversoft. Although both dessert and cooking plums can be cooked, only dessert plums are sweet enough to be eaten raw.

Poaching : Cooking food by simmering in liquid, just below boiling point.

Pochard : A prized variety of duck, having a distinctive and succulent flavour.

Poisson (Fr.) : French name for fish. Do not confuse with poussin.

Polenta (It.) : Corn meal made from maize, which is dried and coarsely ground. Also means Italian Porridge.

Polished Rice : Rice grains with the husk and outer bran layers removed by abrasion with glucose and talc.

Pollack : Similar to cod, but not as white, but is still a useful substitute especially in pies, rissoles, and in fact most 'made-up' dishes.

Polyunsaturated Margarine : Made from vegetable oils instead of fats, so it is lighter in texture and flavour than solid margarine. It spreads very easily, but is not so successful in baking.

Pomace : Residue of fruit or fish pulp from which the oil has been extracted.

Pomegranate : Usually eaten as a raw fruit (the deep red pips are sucked of their juice by mouth and then discarded) though the juice can be extracted mechanically and used as a flavouring in drinks or sweet dishes. The outer skin is bitter and contains tannin.

Pomegranate Seed : (Anardana). The dried seeds of the pomegranate fruit, which can be used to sprinkle on savoury dishes such as Hummus, or included as an ingredient in Parathas or curries.

Pomelo : (Shaddock). The largest of the citrus fruits, and has a thick skin with a bitter fibrous pulp, and of which the grapefruit is a member.

Pomfret : See Bream (sea bream).

Pommes : Botanical name for fruit formed by the enlargement of the receptacle which becomes fleshy and surrounds the carpels e.g. Apples and Pears.

Pone Bread (U.S.) : See Corn Bread.

Pont L'Eveque Cheese (Fr.) : A square, semi-soft pale yellow cheese with a crinkled yellow crust, with a rich, Camembert-like flavour.

Popcorn : A variety of maize that expands greatly on heating.

Pope : (Ruff). Variety of freshwater perch with delicate flesh. Cook as perch.

Popes's Eye : The small circle of fat in the centre of a leg of pork or lamb. Also the name for prime rump steak in Scotland.

Poppadom (Ind.) : Flat, dry pancake, fried in hot oil until crisp. Remove and drain well before serving as an accompaniment to Indian curries.

Poppy Seed : (Kuskus or Mawseed). The seed of the poppy flower, and has a mild nutty flavour and aroma. Often used in Eastern dishes, but also used to garnish pastries, cakes, cheese dishes and various snacks.

Porcupine : An edible animal with rather fatty meat. Best eaten when young.

Pork : Culinary name for pig meat. A versatile meat with a most distinctive flavour. This name normally applies to the uncooked meat, and most cooked and cured pork is known as Ham.

Porridge : A breakfast dish made from boiled oats and salt. Served with milk, cream or syrup.

Port : A fortified Portuguese wine often used as an ingredient in sauces and stocks.

Porter : Beer made from partly charred malt.

Porterhouse Steak : The steak cut from the thick end of the sirloin.

Port-Salut Cheese : A semi-hard, yellow cheese with a reddish rind and a bland taste which ripens with age.

Portuguese Oyster : A variety of oyster that is larger than the normal oyster, with an irregular shell, and has less flavour.

Posset : Drink made from hot milk curdled with ale or wine.

Potage (Fr.) : A cookery term for thick soup.

Potash : An alkaline substance which is vital to the process of nutritional functions.

Potato : Probably the most staple vegetable of the Western World, of which there are many varieties, but only two main types, - early, which are smaller but tastier, and ideal boiled and served hot or cold, or lates, which are the maincrop, and can be stored, (unlike earlies), and are suitable for boiling, baking, frying and roasting. A truly versatile vegetable. Do not confuse with Sweet Potato.

Potato Flour/Starch : (Fecule or Farina). Made from cooked potatoes, dried and ground. It is often used for thickening and adds a subtle flavour to cakes and biscuits where a delicate starch is needed.

Pot Barley : The whole barley grain, which has had only the hard outer husk removed, and is therefore still rich in protein. It takes a good 30 minutes to cook, and can be used on its own or added to soups or stews.

Pot Pourri : A spicy meat stew.

Pot-Roast : To cook food in steam, raised on a rack above a small amount of liquid in a covered pot.

Pottage : A thick stew cooked in a pot over an open fire.

Potted : Refers to cooked meat, poultry or fish that is then ground to a paste and preserved in pots or jars, to be used as a spread on buttered bread.

Pouillard : Name given to young partridge.

Poulette : Describes dishes prepared from previously cooked offal.

Poultry : A term used to describe domestic fowl used for food, including chicken duck, goose and turkey.

Poultry Wing : See Pinion.

Poupeton : Layers of different meats, rolled together and braised.

Poussin (Fr.) : French word for chicken, which should not be confused with poisson.

Pouivron (Fr.) : French name for Pimento.

Praire : See Clam.

Praline (Fr.) : A sweet, consisting of unblanched almonds caramelised in boiling sugar and vanilla. Used to flavour or garnish dessert dishes and cakes.

Pratelle : Variety of large pink mushroom.

Prawn : Small, soft-shelled grey crustaceans, similar to large shrimps, the shells of which turn bright red and the flesh pink when boiled. Normally sold already cooked, with or without their shells. See Shrimps.

Precipitate : In culinary terms. To condense a substance from a liquid solution into a solid form. An extension of reducing.

Preserved Ginger : Young fleshy rhizomes of ginger root, boiled with sugar and packed in syrup.

Preserving : Keeping food in good condition by treating with chemicals, heat, refrigeration, dehydration, pickling in salt, canning, boiling in sugar, or smoking.

Pressure Cooking : A method, using a special hermetically sealed saucepan, to cook food quickly under high pressure steam, which gives an increase in temperature from 100°-130° C. A fast replacement for boiling or braising.

Pretzels (Ger.) : Hard, brittle savoury biscuits made from flour, water, shortening, yeast and salt, which is fermented and then shaped.

Prickly Pear : (Indian Fig). Can be eaten raw or stewed, and is often used in preserves. The thorny skin must be removed before use.

Princesse : Denotes the use of asparagus in a dish.

Printanière (Fr.) : A garnish of spring vegetables, generally shaped into small balls with a scoop.

Processed Cheese : Natural cheese that has been melted and pasteurised, with sometimes flavourings like pimiento or caraway seed added, plus emulsifiers, and then packed. The process arrests the deterioration of natural cheese, and has the same nutritional value, but a different flavour.

Processed Peas : Garden peas that have been matured on the plant and subsequently canned.

Profiteroles : Small rounds of choux pastry used to garnish clear soups, or filled with cream, baked and then topped with a chocolate/syrup sauce.

Promessi (It.) : A soft creamy Italian cheese.

Prosciutto (It.) : Raw smoked ham, finely sliced.

Protein : The part of food needed to supply the body with essential dietary 'amino acids' which are used to re-build body tissues and help defend against infection. The only real sources of 'complete' protein foods are all dairy products, eggs, and soya products such as soya beans, soya milk and soya flour, Tofu, miso and TVP, which are used extensively by certain vegetarians for this very reason. It is important that proteins are obtained on a regular daily basis as there is no body organ capable of storing excess protein. Any surplus intake is expelled in the urine.

Provençal (Fr.) : In the provence style, e.g. cooked with garlic and tomatoes.

Proving: To leave dough in a cool place to mature and rise after shaping. The time taken depends on the mixture, but is normally 15-30 minutes.

Provolone Cheese (It.) : A hard Italian cheese, made in many different shapes, but always tied with string. The thin, smooth rind varies from yellow to white, but the cheese is a creamy-white, which is delicate and sweet to start, but becomes spicy and sharp with ageing. Also available smoked.

Prunes : Preserved red or purple plums that have been sun or oven dried.

Pudding : Baked or boiled sweet dessert, or boiled suet crust which is then filled with meat or poultry.

Puffer : A fritter made from flaked oats, flavoured with cinnamon and fried in butter.

Puff Pastry : (Flaky Pastry). Made by layering fat in dough, which traps the steam when baking, which causes the layers to expand, forming large spaces between them, thus the name.

Pulp : The unprepared soft fleshy tissue of fruit or vegetables reduced to a soft mass by crushing, sieving or boiling. See Purée.

Pulses : The dried seeds of *Legumes* (pod bearing plants), e.g. peas, beans and lentils. Used mainly in vegetarian dishes, but are valuable for their high protein and fibre content.

Pulverised Sugar : Finely powdered sugar.

Pumpernickel : German wholemeal rye bread, with a nearly black crust, and a dark brown crumb. See also black bread.

Pumpkins : A very large, bright orange member of the gourd family. It can be boiled with black pepper and nutmeg, fried, puréed and used in soups, or made into jam. High in vitamin A.

Pumpkin Seed : Mainly used as a source of oil, but can also be deep-fried and toasted, and eaten on their own or used as a nutty garnish.

Punch : A warm alcoholic drink made from spirit or fortified wine, fruit and sugar.

Purée (Fr.) : Raw or cooked food, which has been prepared and then passed through either a sieve, electric blender or liquidiser. See Pulp.

Purgative : A laxative that alters peristaltic (muscular contraction) activity, such as Epsom Salts.

Puri (Ind.) : A thin, circular, wholemeal pancake, similar to chapatis, but are deep-fried in ghee.

Purple Sprouting : A popular variety of broccoli.

Purslane /Purslain : A herb whose young tasty shoots and leaves are eaten raw, in salads.

Quadrille : Thin strips of paste which are laid across open tarts and flans in a decorative fashion.

Quail : A small game bird with little flavour, and should not be hung. Normally stuffed with forcemeat then either roasted or grilled. Allow one bird per person.

Quargel Cheese : A white Austrian cheese with yellow edges, made in small rounds, with a piquant flavour.

Quark : A low-fat curd cheese, which is popular as a health food because of its low saturated fat content. Can be substituted by puréed cottage cheese.

Quart : An Imperial measure equivalent to 2 pints or ¼ gallon.

Quarter : Normally refers to a specific cut or joint of meat.

Quasi : A cut of veal rump.

Quassia : A South American tree whose bitter bark is used in the recipe for an alcoholic tonic drink.

Queensland Nut : See Macadamia nut.

Quenelles (Fr.) : Light savoury dumplings made of meat or fish forcemeat, bound with eggs, and used as a garnish or in a delicate sauce.

Quetch (Fr.) : A plum-flavoured, colourless liqueur.

Quiche (Fr.) : Open-faced pastry case filled with a savoury mixture. See also Guiche.

Quick Breads : A term used for baked goods such as biscuits, muffins, griddles, waffles etc. in which no yeast is used, but the raising is carried out quickly with baking powder, or other chemical agent.

Quick Freezing : A method of rapid freezing of food by exposure to a blast of air at a very low temperature, when small particles of ice are formed, which can be removed by vacuum. The cells of the food are not ruptured, and so the structure is relatively undamaged.

The food is reduced in temperature from 0° to -5° C in under 2 hours, and then cooled to -18°C.

Quinces : (Marmelo). A top fruit with tough golden skin when ripe, and firm acid-flavoured aromatic flesh. Used mainly for making jams and jellies. Rich in pectin. Cannot be eaten raw.

Quinnal (U.S.) : Best quality North American salmon.

Quintal : Variety of cabbage.

Rabbit : A game meat which is similar to, but smaller than, hare, and is prepared and cooked in the same way. It must be skinned immediately after killing, and should not be hung.

Rabiole : Variety of turnip.

Racambole : A small mild-flavoured onion, used mainly raw, in salads, garnishes and pickles.

Racines : A root vegetable used mainly in small quantities as a garnish.

Racoon : Small furred game, cooked as rabbit.

Radiatore (It.) : A dry pasta shaped like an old radiator to 'hold' the sauce.

Radicchio (It.) : A white and maroon leaved variety of chicory, often used in Continental salads. See also rampion.

Radish : The most common variety of this salad vegetable is the small red radish, but there are many others of varying shapes, from round to elongated, and can be red, yellow, black or white. Choose firm ones with bright, well defined colours. See also Daikon.

Raffinade : Best quality refined sugar.

Rafraichir (Fr.) : Literally, to cool or refresh.

Ragoût (Fr.) : A highly seasoned Stew of meat and vegetables, where the meat is browned before adding to the other ingredients.

Raidir : To quickly sear in hot butter or fat.

Rainbow Trout : The most common Trout, normally reared on fish farms. It is green-gold in colour with whitish flesh. Best grilled or baked in foil.

Raised Crust : See Hotwater Pastry.

Raising Powder : See Baking Powder.

Raisins : Dried seedless grapes of which there are several varieties.

Raiton : Small skate.

Ralston (U.S.) : American breakfast cereal of wholewheat with additional wheatgerm.

Ramekins : Individual ovenware dishes, or small pastry cases with cream-cheese filling.

Rampe : See Pandanus.

Rampion : Green-leaved plant, whose roots are cooked as salsify and the leaves as spinach. See radicchio.

Rancid : Normally refers to foods with a high fat content that have begun to enter a state of decomposition, which produces a rank, musty taste and smell.

Rangpar : A red-skinned citrus fruit with orange flesh, the size of a lemon.

Rape : A variety of turnip, grown basically for its oil-producing seeds.

Rape Kale : A variety of Kale that produces young tender shoots, with a strong flavour if overcooked.

Rarebit : See Welsh Rabbit.

Raspberry : A less juicy soft fruit than most, but has a very delicate flavour, and is often sold hulled, and served fresh as a dessert.

Raspings : Very fine stale bread crumbs.

Rastrello : Sharp-edged spoon used to remove pulp from mainly citrus fruit.

Ratafia : Flavouring made from bitter almonds, or a liqueur made from fruit kernels, or a tiny macaroon biscuit used in trifles.

Ratatoullie (Fr.) : Stew made of aubergines, courgettes, onions, peppers and tomatoes cooked in olive oil.

Raton : A type of cheesecake.

Ratonnet : A small skewer of meat.

Ravigote : A highly seasoned white sauce made from green herbs, vinegar and garlic, that can be served hot or cold.

Ravioli (It.) : Small savoury-filled pasta envelopes which are boiled and served with a sauce and grated cheese.

Raw Sugar : Brown unrefined sugar.

Ray : See Skate.

Reblochon Cheese : A pale cream colour soft cheese with an orange rind. It has a bland taste which turns bitter with maturity.

Rechauffer (Fr.) : A term used to describe reheated leftovers.

Recipe : A culinary term to describe the preparation, ingredients and quantities of food needed to produce a specific culinary item.

Reconstituted : Dried food that is returned to its original state by adding water.

Red Bean : (Kidney Bean). Apart from the colour, they are very similar to, and are cooked as French haricot, or French beans.

Red Cabbage : A variety of Cabbage which is beetroot-red in colour, and is used for braising, marinating or pickling raw. Ideal either hot as a vegetable, or cold pickled as a salad dish.

Red Chillies : These small red chillies are extremely pungent. When added to hot oil and fried for a few seconds, they turn dark in colour and give a lovely flavour to the dish. Care should be taken, as they can irritate the eyes and skin.

Red Currants : A bright red glossy berry, which grow in clusters, and are usually sold on their stalks, and then stripped just before serving as a fresh dessert, or in a fruit salad. Excellent for making jelly.

Redfish : See Cardinal.

Red Herring : (Glasgow Magistrate or Yarmouth Bloater). Whole dried and smoked herring, dyed red. It has a strong salty flavour, and is used mainly in mousses and pickles.

Red Kidney Beans : Best known for their use in Mexican spicy dishes such as chilli con carne, but can be added to soups, casseroles, or after cooking, to salads. The skins of these beans contain toxins, which must be removed after soaking and boiling for 10 minutes.

Red Mullet : See Mullet.

Red Pepper : See Pimento.

Reducing : To reduce the volume of a liquid by boiling and evaporation, to concentrate the flavour and thicken its consistency. See also precipitate.

Red Windsor Cheese : A crumbly-textured cheese with the flavour of mild cheddar. No good for cooking.

Refine : A process that improves the quality of a product such as sugar, by removing the impurities, and enhancing its appearance.

Reginette : Very thin wavy variety of noodles.

Regulo : Refers to a scale on gas cookers to indicate the flow of gas to the appliance. The higher the number, the more fierce the flame.

Rehoboam : A bottle equal in size to 6 ordinary bottles, which contains 1 gallon of liquid.

Relish : Sharp or spicy sauce made with fruit or vegetables which adds a piquant flavour to other foods.

Remouillage (Fr.) : The French term to describe a thin, second stock.

Rémoulade : Mayonnaise to which gherkins, capers, onions, tarragon and anchovy essence have been added.

Rendering : Slowly cooking meat tissues and trimmings to obtain fat, dry or wet (with or without water), or clearing fat by heating it.

Renkon (Jap.) : Root of the *Lotus* plant.

Rennet : A substance extracted from animals and in particular the stomach linings of calves, which contains the enzyme rennin, used to precipitate milk for junkets, and for making cheese curd. It can be produced from certain plants such as *Galium Verum* or *Lady's Bedstraw* which is used to make vegetarian cheeses.

Repasse (Fr.) : A French term to 'repeatedly strain', which process is mainly used in the preparation of fine sauces.

Rhizome : A root-like stem that grows along, or under the soil, with edible roots and shoots.

Rhubarb : A plant whose leaves are highly poisonous and should be safely discarded. Early or forced rhubarb has tender, pink and delicately flavoured stalks which do not require peeling. Maincrop stalks have a stronger flavour, and should be 'stringed' in a similar manner to celery. Normally stewed with sugar and a little water, but may be added to pies or crumbles or made into jam or wine. Avoid limp stalks.

Ribbon : Used to describe a wavy line of well-beaten sugar and egg yolk mixture, draped in a band across various preparations, normally cakes and desserts.

Rib of Beef : The joints of beef from the rib area, of which there are various parts; top, fore, back, flat and wing, of which the latter is the most preferred joint.

Riboflavin : (Vitamin G) The water soluble vitamin B, found mainly in liver and dairy products.

Rice : The most staple grain in the world, of which there are very many varieties, and are low in fat, high in gluten, and basically fall into two main types; long grain and short grain. Long grain rice has dry, separate grains when cooked and is nearly always used in Indian cookery. Short grain rice tends to have a stickier, softer texture, and is more popular in Oriental and European cookery and desserts. Western countries tend to use white refined rice, or easy-cook rice, though this is the least nutritious of all. Other main varieties include brown rice, which takes longer to cook than white, and is mainly associated with health food and vegetarian dishes. See Basmati, Patna, Arborio, Short-grain and Wild Rice.

Rice Flakes : Apart from the whole grain, rice is also available in the form of flakes (either brown or white), which is used to make a variety of muesli and also a rice porridge.

Rice Flour : A gluten-free flour made from both brown and white rice. It is used mainly in Oriental cookery for making noodles, cakes and biscuits. It can also be used as a thickening agent.

Rice Paper : Edible, glossy white paper made from the pith of a tree grown in China. Used for a macaroon base.

Rice Patna : See Patna rice.

Rice Wine : See Saké.

Ricing : Culinary term for cutting or chopping into small pieces the size of rice grains.

Ricotta Cheese (It.) : A soft, bland Italian cheese with a distinctly ridged rind. Made from sheep's milk, salt and lemon juice. It has a low fat content and is mainly used for cooking in dishes such as lasagna.

Riddle : A large-holed, coarse sieve.

Ridge Cucumber : A type of cucumber cultivated in the open, compared to the normal 'house' or 'frame' varieties. It has the same flavour, but generally smaller and less attractive, therefore normally used for cooking and pickling, rather than for salads.

Rigatoni (It.) : Ribbed elbow-shaped macaroni.

Rigg : See Huss.

Rind : Normally refers to the outer skin of meat and cheese. See also Peel.

Riso Cristallo : See Crystal Rice or Wildrice.

Risotto (It.) : Savoury short-grained rice based dish, fried and then cooked in stock or tomato juice and finished with cheese.

Rissole : Small roll or patty made of puff pastry filled with forcemeat, and deep-fried.

River Trout : (Brown Trout). An oily fish with a superior flesh to the rainbow trout, with a dark spotted skin. Ideal for grilling or frying.

Roach : Very fine-boned variety of carp, whose white flesh turns red during cooking.

Roasting : Cooking in the oven with radiant heat, or on a spit over or under an open flame.

Roasting Chicken : (Broiler). A popular sized bird weighing about 3-4lbs., and young enough at 6-12 months to be suitable for grilling, frying or roasting. Available whole, jointed and fresh or frozen.

Rocambole : (Tree Onion) A member of the onion family whose fruit grows at the top of its stems.

Rock Eel : See Huss.

Rocket : A piquant variety of cress, used in salads.

Rockfish : See Catfish.

Rock Lobster : See Crayfish.

Rock Partridge : A top class variety of European partridge.

Rock Salmon : See Coley.

Rock Salt : A basic salt obtained from underground deposits, similar to Table Salt but less refined.

Rock Sugar : Amber-coloured sugar crystals, used for sweetening desserts and sweet teas.

Roe : Either milt or sperm of the male fish, called soft roe, or eggs of the female fish, called hard roe, or shellfish roe, called coral because of its colour.

Roebuck : Alternative name for deer.

Rokelax (Sca.) : Scandinavian term for Smoked Salmon.

Rolled Oats : See Oat flakes.

Roll Mop : Herring fillet marinated in spiced vinegar, and rolled round chopped onion, gherkins and peppers.

Romaine : See Cos.

Romano (It.) : In the style of Rome.

Root : A term used to describe vegetables whose underground parts are swollen, and used as culinary ingredients.

Root Ginger : See Ginger.

Roquefort Cheese : A crumbly blue cheese with a salty but piquant flavour. It is made from ewe's milk curds, sprinkled with breadcrumbs, and specially treated with mould to make the characteristic green veins.

Rose Hips : Fruit of the *Rose* plant, and used mainly to produce rosehip syrup. Rich in vitamin C.

Rosemary : A favourite herb, which is delicately sweet and fragrant, and often used with oily grilled fish, and to flavour roast lamb, pork, duck and goose. May also be added to casseroled potatoes. Available fresh, dried or powdered, but the needle-shaped are normally used on the sprig, and a common ingredient of bouquet garnis or a garnish for vegetable dishes.

Rose Water : Has a delicate fragrance and is used for flavouring Indian dishes. Available as an essence but is quite expensive.

Rôtie (Fr.) : Slice of baked or toasted bread.

Roti Flour (Ind.) : A creamy, slightly granular flour used for unleavened bread. Unlike Atta flour, it is not made from the whole grain.

Rôtisserie (Fr.) : Rotating spit used for grilling meat, fish or poultry, either whole, or in quarters or skewered.

Rougail : A highly-spiced Creole condiment.

Roughage : An old term for Dietary Fibre.

Rouille : Garlic, tomato purée, breadcrumbs and chilli combined to make a paste. Often served with Bouillabaisse.

Roulade (Fr.) : Roll of meat, vegetables, chocolate cake etc.

Round (U.S.) : See Silverside.

Round Garden Peas : A variety of green pea that remains round even when dried. They are more tender and smaller than the wrinkled varieties, and if required fresh, they are available in the spring, being the early crop pea. Available fresh, dried, frozen or canned.

Round Lettuce : (Cabbage Lettuce). Soft-leaved round lettuce, available all year, but has less flavour than summer varieties. See Cos.

Roux (Fr.) : Mixture of flour and butter or fat which is lightly cooked, to which warm milk or stock may be added. The mixture is boiled and then used as a basis for savoury sauces or for thickening gravies or soups.

Royal : Fine icing, made from icing sugar and egg whites.

Royan : A type of large sardine.

Rubbing In : A method of combining fat and flour together by gently rubbing between the fingers to form a short texture for pastry, cakes and biscuits.

Rudd : A rather tasteless fish of the roach family, used mainly in soups.

Ruff : See Pope.

Rum : Spirit produced from cane sugar.

Rumen : A term to describe animals (such as cows, sheep and goats), with four stomachs, humans having one.

Rump : Fleshy part of a haunch of beef.

Runner Beans : A popular type of green bean, similar to but larger and coarser than the French bean, but with more flavour. The fresh beans are cooked and eaten with their pods, but unless very young and small, the pods are stringed and sliced into 2 inch diagonal lengths before boiling. The pods should snap easily when bought, so avoid limp or mishapen beans. Suitable for freezing sliced, but the beans are not used separately, fresh, like French or broad beans.

Rusk : Normally purchased item made from slices of special bread which is re-baked to produce a form of light toast or biscuit.

Russet Apple : A rough-skinned dessert apple with a smooth flesh and delicious flavour.

Russet Pear : Dessert pear with a sweet-flavoured flesh and a matt finished skin.

Russian Dressing : Mayonnaise dressing which includes chilli sauce, worcester sauce and many various seasonings.

Rutabaga (U.S.) : American term for Swede vegetable. See Swede.

Rye : A strong-flavoured grain, which in the culinary world is used as cracked grain or as flakes that are normally lightly toasted.

Rye Flour : A greyish flour that darkens easily and is the main ingredient in Black Bread, but is also excellent for making some crispbreads and pancakes. This is a gluten-free flour.

Saccharine : A chemical sweetening agent with no food value. Mainly used by diabetics and slimmers.

Saddle : The undivided loin from a meat carcass, extending from the last ribs to the leg on both sides.

Saffron : A delicate honey-flavoured spice with a beautiful yellow colour. It is very expensive and can be substituted by tumeric (haldi). It is made from the dried stigmas of the crocus flower, hence the cost. A traditional ingredient of the Spanish dish 'paella', and Indian pilau and biryani dishes. Can be bought as a filaments or as a powder. See Curcuma.

Sage : A bold, penetrating, fragrant, spicy herb, mainly used in stuffings for pork, chicken and duck. Also used to flavour oily fish, especially eel, and various forcemeats. Aids digestion.

Sage Derby Cheese : A variety of Derby cheese which has chopped sage incorporated to enhance the flavour.

Sago : Starchy reddish-yellow grains prepared from the pith of the *Sago* Palm. Virtually pure starch. Used extensively in dietary dishes.

Saignant (Fr.) : French term for underdone meat. Literally 'bloody'.

Saingorlon Cheese (Fr.) : A sharp blue cheese, which is very similar to Gorgonzola.

Saint John's Bread : See Carob Powder.

Saint Marcellin Cheese (Fr.) : A small round crumbly cheese, made from goats' milk, with a mild, slightly salty taste.

Saint Nectaire Cheese (Fr.) : A semi-hard pale yellow cheese, with a mottled rind, and a bland subtle flavour.

Saint Pauline Cheese (Fr.) : A semi-hard yellow cheese with a bland taste similar to port-salut.

Saithe : See Coley.

Sakazuki (Jap.) : Wine cup.

Saké/Saki (Jap.) : The national alcoholic drink of Japan. A mild-tasting but potent rice wine, which is normally drunk warm. Also used as a cooking ingredient. Can be substituted by dry sherry.

Salad : Probably the most varied natural dish in the culinary world. Prepared from plants, meat, fish, vegetables, eggs, and herbs. The mixtures are seasoned with salt, pepper, vinegar or oil and various prepared dressings.

Salad Cream : Oil-in-water emulsion, consisting of vegetable oil, vinegar, salt and spices, which are mixed and then emulsified with eggyolk.

Salad Dressing : See French Dressing.

Salad Onion : See Scallion.

Salamander : An over-fired grill producing radiant heat under which is a metal barred frame on which food is placed to be grilled *under heat.* A tray may also be placed beneath the Salamander bars to hold small items of food such as tomatoes, mushrooms, bacon etc. The Salamander can also be used to brown or glaze certain dishes.

Salami (It.) : Spiced beef and/or pork sausage, which is sold fresh or smoked.

Salmi (Fr.) : Stew, first made by roasting game and then cooking in wine sauce.

Salmon : A superior saltwater fish, but is caught in freshwater rivers on its way to spawn. It should have bright silvery scales, red gills and pink-red close textured flesh, and weighing from 8 - 12 lbs. Can be purchased whole or as steaks. It needs only very gentle poaching or baking, and is normally served cold, with various dressings and sauces. Available smoked, but is a definite luxury. Can also be pickled raw, as in gravalax.

Salmonella : A Bacteria which is the main cause of food poisoning, often found with infected eggs and sausages etc., which can survive in brine and/or chilled temperatures. It must be destroyed by adequate heating and cooking.

Salmon Trout : Variety of trout with pink coloured flesh like salmon.

Salpicon : A term used to describe a preparation of one or more small diced ingredients combined with a sauce and used to fill pastry cases etc.

Salsa : Piquant sauce with onions, tomatoes, peppers and chillies.

Salsify : (Oyster Plant). Long, delicately flavoured white roots from a plant of the *Compositae* family. Similar in appearance to a thin parsnip. Used in soups, salads and savoury dishes. Normally grated and sprinkled with lemon juice to prevent discoloration. See Scarzonera and Wild Salsify.

Salt : One of the most traditional of food flavourings is the mineral sodium chloride which is extracted either from the sea or from underground deposits. There are various types of salt, the most common being: table salt, rock salt and sea salt. There are also flavoured salts available such as onion and garlic, which are simply basic salt with additives.

Salted Cabbage : Pungent and greenish-brown in colour, sold in bundles, and used to flavour meat, fish and soup dishes. Soak or rinse well before use.

Salt Herring : Whole or gutted herring preserved in heavy salt brine, which usually needs soaking for 24 hours before preparing for use.

Salting : Preserving food, mainly meat in layers of salt. It is also a term used to sprinkle certain sliced vegetables such as aubergines and courgettes with salt, then leave for about an hour before rinsing under cold water. This process reduces the natural water content in the vegetables which aids cooking and more importantly their digestion.

Saltpetre : A chemical (potassium nitrate) used in very small amounts as a preservative for curing meat. Also gives a redness to the meat.

Sambal Ulek (Ind.) : A salty and extremely hot paste made from fresh chillies and salt.

Sambol (Ind.) : General name given to a curry of fairly thick consistency.

Samna (Egypt.) : See Ghee.

Samp : Coarsely cracked maize with the bran and germ partly removed.

Samphire : (Peter's Cress, Sea Fennel). Eaten as fennel, or pickled in vinegar.

Samshu (Chin.) : Chinese rice beer.

Samsoe Cheese (Dan.) : A mild-flavoured Danish cheese with a sweet, nutty taste. Yellow, with a firm texture and shiny round eyes.

Sand Eel : Small fish found on sandy beaches, and cooked as smelt.

Sand-Smelt : See Athérine.

Sandwich : A snack made from two slices of buttered bread with either a savoury filling or sweet preserve spread.

Sangaree : A West Indian punch made from port, lime juice, sugar and spices.

Sanguine : See Blood Orange.

Sansho (Jap.) : Crushed Japanese pepper made from the seeds of the prickly *Ash* tree. It has a mild flavour, and used for seasoning.

Santarosa : A type of plum.

Sapodilla : (Naseberry Plum). A fruit the size of a small apple, rough-grained, with a yellow-grey pulp.

Saracen Corn : See Buckwheat.

Sardine : A small saltwater fish, similar to herring or pilchard. Does not keep at all well, so is normally sold tinned in oil or tomato, or if fresh, it is sold slightly salted.

Sargasso : Variety of seaweed eaten in salads.

Sarsaparilla : A flavouring obtained from aromatic oils, and mainly used in carbonated drinks.

Sashimi (Jap.) : Japanese term for raw seafood.

Sassafras (U.S.) : A drink made by the infusion of the leaves, buds and bark of the *Laurel* tree.

Satoimo (Jap.) : See Eddoe.

Satsuma : A round squat orange, similar to a tangerine, with smooth, yellowish fairly thick skin, and pale orange-yellow flesh with no pips. Use as a fresh dessert, or to make marmalade.

Satsumaimo (Jap.) : See Sweet Potato.

Sauce : A specialised area of culinary arts and too varied to describe in detail. This term is used to describe any form of prepared liquid that is either added to food during cooking, or poured over a main dish just before serving. The various sauces may often be served hot or cold.

Saucisson : Large, savoury sausages that are served as cut slices.

Sauerkraut (Pol.) : Shredded cabbage with salt, that has been prepared by lactic fermentation, and flavoured with juniper berries.

Saurel : (Horse Mackerel). A long round fish, resembling and cooked as mackerel.

Sausage : Either a mixture of raw lean and fat meat - normally pork, seasonings and additives, which are encased in a skin, and normally grilled or fried. Or a mixture of cold meats and ingredients that have already been cooked, smoked and/or cured to produce a multitude of savoury meat products, too numerous to mention by name.

Sauté (Fr.) : To fry food rapidly in a deep sided frying pan, in shallow hot fat, tossing and turning it until evenly browned.

Sauterne : A naturally sweetened white wine from Bordeaux, much used in various culinary dishes.

Savarin (Fr.) : Rich yeast cake, which is baked in a ring mould and soaked in liqueur-flavoured syrup. Served cold with cream.

Saveloy : A highly seasoned smoked sausage. Can be eaten hot or cold.

Savory : An aromatic herb with a minty flavour. Summer savory has a more delicate mint flavour than winter savory. Both are used to flavour salads and soups, grilled fish and egg dishes. Especially good with runner beans.

Savouries : Similar to hors d'oeuvres, but are generally served after a main meal and vary greatly in the ingredients used, but often include cheese as a main constituent, on a toast base.

Savoy Cabbage : A popular winter Cabbage with crisp, puckered dark green leaves.

Saxifrages : A group of fleshy-leaved plants used as a vegetable or in soups.

Scald : To heat milk or cream to just below boiling point, or to plunge fruit or vegetables in boiling water to ease the removal of the skins. Also a defect in stored apples which causes browning. See also Blanching.

Scale : Either the thin, hard, layered 'petals' that protect the skin of fish and reptiles, or their removal during food preparation.

Scallion : (Salad, Bunch, Green or Spring Onions). Small white-skinned, mild-flavoured variety of onion, with dark green leaves, developed specifically for use in salads or as a garnish. Can be substituted by shallots when not in season, or the young 'thinnings' of the bulb onion varieties.

Scallop : Edible mollusc with white flesh and orange coral or roe. The deep fluted shell can be used for serving the scallops and other foods. Can be grilled, poached or lightly sauteed, but must always be cooked tenderly and quickly, or the flesh will become tough. There is a smaller variety known as Queens.

Scalloping : Decorating the edge of a pastry pie by making small cuts around the edge and pulling up with a cold knife to produce a 'scalloped' effect.

Scalloppine (It.) : Small escalopes of veal, weighing 30 gm and about 3in. square.

Scampi : See Dublin Bay Prawn.

Scarlet Runner : See Runner Bean.

Scarole : A broad-leaved variety of chicory.

Scarus : See Parrot Fish.

Schaleth : A Jewish apple pie made with noodle paste in place of puff pastry.

Schlosskäse (Aus.) : A mild-flavoured soft Austrian cheese, pale yellow in colour, with a heavily creased rind.

Schnitzel (Ger.) : Veal slices coated in egg and crumbs, then fried in butter. See Escalope.

Scone : A variety of small cake, made from oatmeal and sour milk, named after Scone in Scotland, from where it originated.

Scoring : Cutting gashes or narrow grooves in the surface of food, e.g. in pork to produce crackling, or making a pattern of squares or diamonds on pastry crust.

Scorzonera : The black-skinned variety of salsify.

Scotch Eggs : Hard-boiled eggs surrounded by a layer of sausage meat, then egg-and-crumbed and deep-fried.

Scotch Oats : Groats that have been cut into granules.

Scoter-Duck : Variety of duck with oily, strong flavoured flesh. Use young birds only.

Screwpine : See Pandanus.

Scrod : Young Cod.

Scum : The froth that appears on the surface of boiling food preparations, or the skin that forms on the top of a liquid substance when cold.

Sea Anemone : See Actinia.

Sea Bass : See Bass.

Sea Bream : See Bream.

Sea-Cow (W.I.) : (Manatee). Sea mammal, whose flesh tastes similar to pork.

Sea Cucumber : See Beche-de-Mer.

Sea Dace : See Bass.

Sea Eel : See Conger Eel.

Sea Fennel : See Samphire.

Seafoods : Generally refers to all varieties of crustaceans and shellfish.

Seakale : A vegetable of the cabbage species, grown for its shoots, which are forced, then blanched, and cooked like asparagus or cardoons.

Seakale Beet : See Swiss Chard.

Seal : To brown meat rapidly, usually in fat, for flavour and colour.

Sea Perch : See Bass.

Searing : Browning meat rapidly with fierce heat to seal in the juices, prior to grilling or roasting. See also Raidir.

Sea Salt : Strong-flavoured crystals obtained from evaporated sea water, used in small quantities for cooking.

Sea Slug : See Beche-de-Mer.

Seasoned Flour : Flour flavoured with salt and pepper, used to dust meat or fish prior to cooking.

Season : Of food, to flavour, generally with salt and pepper, either before or after its preparation. See also Flavouring.

Sea Trout : A freshwater fish with silvery scales, a firm pale-pink flesh and a delicate flavour similar to salmon. Always sold whole, and cooked as salmon.

Sea Urchin : (Oursin) A spiny-shelled marine animal, eaten raw, or lightly boiled or poached.

Sea Vegetables : These vegetables are a common ingredient in Oriental cooking, but are becoming popular in the West. Depending on the variety, they can be boiled, grilled, stir-fried or added to soups, stews or salads. Only a little is needed as they expand considerably when soaked. See headings such as Arame, Hiziki, Carrageen etc. for descriptions and uses.

Seaweed : A leafy variety of sea vegetable from the Orient. See headings such as dulse, kombu, wakame, kelp etc. for descriptions and uses.

Sea Wolf : See Bass.

Sec (Fr.) : A wine term meaning 'dry'.

Seedcake : The residue of oil seeds after the oil has been extracted. Rich in protein.

Seedless Raisins : See Sultanas.

Seed Sprout : A term used to cover any seeds that are used to produce seedlings, which are cut and eaten raw or cooked, like mustard and cress or bean sprouts. High in nutritional value.

Seitan : A vegetarian dough made from plain flour, salt and water.

Self-Raising Flour : (Aerated flour) A fine, white wheat flour with baking powder added to act as a leavening agent. It should be used soon after purchase, as its potency declines, especially in damp conditions.

Semolina : A product made from the starchy part (endosperm) of durum wheat grain. Although mainly used to make pasta and couscous, it is also used in gnocchi and various milky desserts. Available refined or unrefined.

Senbei (Jap.) : Salted Japanese cracker.

Sereh Powder : A dried powdered version of lemon grass.

Serendipity Berry : An extremely sweet-tasting West African berry.

Serviette : A linen or paper cloth provided to diners for protecting their clothing and for wiping their hands and mouth during meals. Can also be used to hold certain solid foodstuffs during consumption.

Sesame Jam : Has a very nutty flavour, being made from sesame oil and peanut butter.

Sesame Oil : A nutty flavoured oil, and used in small quantities for its aromatic qualities and not as a cooking medium. The Chinese product is made from toasted seeds and gives a stronger flavour than the oil of the same name that is available in health food stores. See also Toasted Sesame Oil.

Sesame Salt : See Gomasio.

Sesame Seeds : Small creamy-yellow flat seeds, normally roasted to bring out their nutty flavour, and used in cake or dessert mixtures to give a nutty aroma.

Set : In culinary terms, to coagulate a liquid preparation by either heating or chilling.

Seville Orange (Sp) : See Bitter Orange.

Shad : A fish, similar in size and taste to herrings, but contains a numerous amount of bones. The female has the better flesh, but the male is popular for its soft roe. Cook as herring.

Shad-Bush : A tree whose fruit is slightly tart, and best when overripe.

Shaddock : A citrus fruit. See Pomelo.

Shallots : A small, sharp-tasting variety of onion, which can be used in savoury dishes, soups and stews. Can be used as a substitute for scallions. They grow in clusters, like garlic, and have a similar shape.

Shallow-Fry : See Frying.

Shark's Fin (Chin.) : Hard, dried pieces of shark cartilage, greyish-brown in colour. Must be well soaked, and needs prolonged cooking, either braised, or included in a thick soup. It becomes translucent when cooked.

Sharon Fruit : See Persimmon.

Sharpen : In culinary terms, to render a liquid more acid, by the addition of lemon juice or citric acid.

Shashlik : Identical to shishkebab, but without marinating in wine.

Shchi (Russ.) : The Russian national soup, which is made mainly from cabbage.

Shea Butter : A vegetable butter, which is softer than coconut butter.

Shearling : Sheep that are 15 - 18 months old.

Sheep : The flesh of which, is known as mutton. Flesh of sheep under 15 months is known as lamb.

Shell Bean (U.S.) : See Broad Bean.

Shellfish : A form of live edible seafood, that is divided into two main groups; Crustaceans, which have jointed shells, like crabs, lobsters and shrimps; and molluscs, which have hinged shells, like mussels, oysters and scallops. Much confusion exists over the names of shellfish, but see individual headings for correct descriptions and name choices, e.g. Dublin Bay Prawn, Langoustine, Scampi.

Shellfish Roe : See Coral Roe.

Sherbet : (Sorbet). Refreshing water-ice made from water, sugar and flavouring. See Granités.

Sherry : A fortified Spanish wine used in many food recipes to enhance the flavour.

Shichimi (Jap.) : A mixture of spices varying in strength. Can be substituted with paprika.

Shin of Beef : The forepart of a leg of beef, used mainly in broths and soups.

Shioyaki (Jap.) : Broiling in salt.

Shirataki (Jap.) : Translucent noodles made from the threads of gelatinous starch extracted from a root vegetable, known as *Devil's Tongue.*

Shiratamako (Jap.) : A mixture of mochi and rice flour.

Shiru-Miso (Jap.) : Soup made with miso.

Shishkebab : Cubed lamb or beef, marinated in onion, garlic and wine, then skewered alternately with vegetables like tomatoes, mushrooms, capsicum etc..

Shitake (Jap.) : Dried Japanese tree mushrooms. Can be substituted with fresh mushrooms.

Shortbread : A Scottish, fairly thick, sweet, crumbly biscuit made from short pastry.

Shortening : Term for an edible fat used in certain pastry and cake preparation.

Short Grain Rice : Small, chalky, oval-grained rice which absorbs a large quantity of liquid during cooking, and produces a sticky mass. Used mainly for desserts and Oriental dishes. See also Arborio.

Short Pastry : Describes a pastry dough where basically half the amount of butter by weight is added to the weight of flour. See Puff Pastry.

Shoyu Sauce (Jap.) : A light sauce which should not be confused with or substituted by any Chinese or other soy sauces, as the flavour is completely different, and will spoil the dish.

Shredding : Slicing vegetables very thinly, in particular potatoes and carrots. Fluted shredders produce vegetable ribbons. See Grating.

Shrimp : A crustacean often mistaken for prawn, but is much smaller. Normally bought cooked, they can be eaten whole in their shells, or peeled and incorporated into sauces, soups, salads and stews. The common or brown shrimp has a grey-brown soft shell which turns only slightly pinkish when boiled, and are much tastier than the pink shrimp which has a grey shell that turns rosy-pink when boiled. See Prawn.

Shrimp Paste : See Dried Shrimp Paste.

Shrimp Sauce : A highly savoury sauce, used to flavour fish dishes or soups. Also used in dips.

Shungiku (Jap.) : Edible chrysanthemum leaf with a similar texture and colour to spinach, but with a much milder flavour, and imparts a subtle fragrance to soups and delicate dishes.

Sichuan Brown Peppercorns : Peppery, aromatic red-brown dried berries, which are vital to the characteristic taste of Sichuan dishes.

Sieving : Passing flour or sugar through a sieve to remove lumps, and achieve a soft, even texture.

Sifting : Another name for sieving.

Sild : Young Herrings.

Silica Gel : A Drying Agent.

Silver Chard : See Swiss Chard.

Silver Hake : See Whiting.

Silver Leaf : (Varak). Thin silver leaf used to decorate both sweet and savoury dishes.

Silverside (Beef) : (Round). A joint of beef that includes the tendons, biceps and gemelus muscle. Normally braised, and bought larded, rolled and tied. Can be either salted or unsalted.

Silverside (Fish) : See Athérine.

Simmering : Cooking in liquid which is heated to just below boiling point, with faint ripples on the surface, a condition essential for poaching.

Singeing : Burning off with a lighted taper, any remaining traces of feathers on plucked poultry, birds or game.

Single Gloucester : A less mature Gloucester cheese than Double Gloucester, with a mellow, creamy taste, and a soft, open texture. Ideal for grilling.

Siphon : Container for holding liquid under pressure from carbonic gas like Soda Water.

Sippets : Small pieces of bread, similar to croûtons, fried or toasted and used to garnish mince or hash.

Sirloin : The meat section between the hook and first rib, which includes the fillet, sirloin and rump steaks.

Sirop : Syrup produced by cooking fruit in sugar until it is reduced to a thick liquid.

Skate : (Ray). A good tasting, flat, scaleless fish with pink flesh, but only the 'wings' with their prominent bones are sold. Must be carefully poached, preferably in a well-flavoured fish or wine stock, or lightly shallow fried. One of the few fish that keeps reasonably well.

Skewer : Metal or wooden pin used to hold meat, poultry or fish in shape during cooking, normally under a grill.

Skillet : A medium depth frying pan with a lid.

Skimming : Removing cream from the surface of milk, or fat, froth or scum from the surface of stock, stews, broth or jam.

Skinning : To remove the skin of certain game, fish and fowl. The removal of the outer skin of fruit and vegetables is known as Peeling.

Skirret : Name for a variety of mushroom.

Slake : To mix flour, arrowroot, cornflour or custard powder to a thin paste with a small quantity of cold water.

Slaughter : To kill an animal for meat. The various methods used depend on the type of animal, and can affect the appearance and quality of the meat produced.

Sleeve-Fish : See Squid.

Sliver : A thin slice of bread, meat, vegetable or cheese or any solid food substance.

Sloe : A wild sour plum from the *Blackthorn*. Mainly used in the production of gin or jam.

Smelt : (Sparling). Tiny saltwater fish which, like salmon, spawns and is caught in rivers. It has pure white flesh with a strong aroma, but delicate flavour. Grill, shallow or deep-fry. See Athérine and Sand Eel.

Smetana : A low-fat sour cream which can be used as a substitute for healthy or sour cream in savoury dishes.

Smoked Haddock : Haddock that is smoked until pale yellow. Avoid very yellow pieces as they are probably artificially coloured and have less flavour. See Finnan Haddock and Arbroath Smokies.

Smoked Salmon : Scotch salmon has strips of fat between the meat, and is considered to be the finest type.

Smoked Trout : Rainbow trout which is smoked to a dark brown colour. Requires no cooking.

Smoking : Curing food, such as meat, bacon or fish, by exposing it to hardwood smoke for a considerable period of time, which dries and also sterilizes the food.

Smörgasbärd (Scand.) : Scandinavian table laid with buffet style delicacies like fish, meat or cheese.

Smörrebräd (Dan.) : Danish open sandwich - literally means 'smeared bread'.

Snail : (Escargot). Common name for a land mollusc, very much favoured in French cuisine, and has an acquired and very succulent taste. They are prepared and eaten either in or out of their shells, normally combined with liberal amounts of wine, herbs and garlic.

Snake Gourd : A variety of gourd which is a member of the marrow and squash family.

Snap Beans : See French Beans.

Snibbing : Topping and tailing of fruit like gooseberries. See also Nubbing.

Snipe : An uncommon small game bird, which is normally roasted.

Snowball : A dessert made from chocolate ice-cream, vanilla mousse and crystallized fruit.

Snow Eggs : Shaped mounds of stiffly whipped egg-whites and sugar poached in milk.

Snow Pea : See Mangetout.

Soak : To immerse in water for a period of time. Normally applies to dried fruit, vegetables and salted meat in readiness for their preparation.

Soba (Jap.) : Slender noodles made from buckwheat flour.

Soda Bread : A loaf that is leavened with sodium bicarbonate and acid in place of yeast.

Soda Water : Carbonated water which is added to fruit juices and alcoholic drinks.

Softening : (Bletting). A term used to describe the overripeness of fruit, verging on a state of rotting. Some fruits, such as medlor or persimmon, are rather tart, unpleasant and inedible until bletted, whereas with fruit such as apples and pears, softening is a sign of decay and can be very unpleasant.

Soft Fruits : This term covers all fruits which are best used on the day of purchase, and are normally sold loose in punnets or containers, and generally, can cause stains. Avoid mushy or squashed fruits.

Soft Roe : The smooth white sperm of the male fish, normally lightly poached. See Roe.

Sole (Dover) : A superb flat fish, with white, firm delicate flesh, which is best when lightly poached or grilled with the minimum of seasoning or sauces, but preferably just accompanied by a wedge of lemon, potatoes and side salad. Can be cooked whole or filleted.

Sole (Lemon) : Although of slightly less quality than the Dover sole, it is still a very good fish, and can be treated in exactly the same manner as its counterpart. Probably best grilled or baked on the bone.

Somen (Jap.) : Fine wheatflour noodles which can be substituted by vermicelli.

Sop : Another name for Bread.

Sorbet (Fr.) : Water ice made with fruit juice or puree. See also Sherbet.

Sorghum : A cereal that is a form of millet, grown in tropical countries, and mainly used for porridge and flatcakes.

Sorrel (Fr.) : The tender green leaves look and taste like spinach, but with a slightly bitter, sharp flavour, and the leaves can be cooked whole or puréed, but should only be eaten in small quantities as they are high in oxalic acid. Only available fresh. When used as a herb, it makes an excellent addition to salads, or as a flavouring in soups, omelettes and sauces. It should be cooked for the shortest time possible to preserve its flavour. Do not cook in iron containers as it will turn black.

Soufflé (Fr.) : A baked sweet or savoury dish consisting of a sauce or purée, which is thickened with egg yolks into which stiffly beaten egg whites are folded in just before cooking.

Souffle Dish : Straight-sided dish used for cooking and serving souffles.

Soup : Normally the first course of a meal, which can be clear, thick, velouté or cream, the flavour of which should set the tone of the main course.

Sour : An ingredient, preparation or dish that possesses an acidic, piquant taste or smell.

Sour Cream : Cream to which citric acid has been added - in the form of the substance itself, or normally lemon juice, to give it a sour taste.

Sour Sop : See Custard Apple.

Sousing : Pickling food - usually fish, in brine or vigegar, e.g. soused herrings.

Soya Bean / Soybean : Regarded in the Far East as 'The meat of the Earth'. They are extremely versatile, yielding many products, and are unique among beans in that they contain the eight essential amino acids thus providing complete protein. The beans themselves can be either yellow or black, and available whole, dried or fermented. Can be cooked in stews, mixed with other legumes and pulses, but are best known for their by-products, such as soy sauce, tofu (bean curd), miso, tempeh, soya grits and flakes.

Soyabean Curd : See Tofu.

Soya Flakes : A product of soya beans that are processed in much the same way that oats are rolled.

Soya Flour : Made from dried soya beans, it is used as a nutritious supplement to soups, cakes and breads, and should not be confused with conventional flour.

Soya Grit : Similar to soya flakes, but smaller particles.

Soya Meat : A normally purchased item, regarded as 'vegetarian meat', that has the appearance and flavour of cooked ham.

Soya Milk : An extract from soya beans which is available in liquid or dried forms. It has a pleasant nutty flavour, which can be used as a substitute for cows milk, especially in certain dishes such as soups to enhance the flavour, but it is not recommended in tea or coffee.

Soya Sauce (Chin.) : A salty brown sauce, which adds flavour to meat, poultry, fish or vegetable dishes. A versatile sauce, used mainly with Chinese dishes. The darker the sauce, the stronger the flavour. See Shoyu sauce and Tamari Soy.

Spaghetti (It.) : Versatile and nutritious Italian pasta of various thickness and shapes of solid strands, compared with macaroni which is hollow tubes.

Spaghetti : A variety of squash, which is a member of the marrow, gourd and squash family.

Spare Ribs : Generally applies to the ribs of pork that are separated from the side of the back, which have very little meat and are normally marinaded before frying and eaten from the bone.

Sparling : See Smelt.

Sparrowgrass : A slang name for asparagus.

Spices : Usually refers to the whole or ground aromatic seeds and/or pods of plants in comparison to herbs, which are considered to be the stems and leaves of aromatic plants, both of which are used to flavour culinary preparations.

Spinach : A green-leaf vegetable high in iron content. The summer variety is less coarse and bitter tasting than the winter variety, and is so tender that it can be eaten raw in salads. Both types can be boiled or steamed on their own as a vegetable dish or used as stuffings in pancakes and fillings in quiches and savoury flans. The leaves reduce greatly in volume during cooking so purchase ample quantities. See Good King Henry.

Spinach Beet : See Swiss Chard.

Spiny Lobster : See Crayfish.

Spirit : A strong alcoholic drink, produced by the distillation of various already fermented liquids, thus producing the high percentage of alcohol.

Spit : Revolving skewer or metal rod on which meat, poultry, game or fish is roasted over a fire or barbecue, or under a grill or salamander.

Split Lentils : Dried lentils that are naturally halved.

Split Pea Flour : Made from dried and ground yellow split peas, and can be used to thicken soups and stews. Cannot be used as a conventional grain flour.

Split Peas : Green or Yellow dried peas that are naturally halved.

Sprat : A small oily silver-skinned saltwater fish, similar in appearance to a small herring, and of the same species. Ideal for grilling, frying, barbecues or baking. Available fresh or smoked. See also Brisling.

Spring Cabbage : A variety of cabbage which provides tender spring greens, and mature heads later in the year. Generally conical in shape and smaller than the summer and winter varieties.

Spring Chicken : Young chickens about 3 months old, and weighing about 2-3 lbs. Best roasted. Serves 2 persons.

Spring-Form Mould : Baking tin with hinged sides, held together by a metal clamp or pin, which is opened to release the cake or pie.

Spring Onions : See Scallion.

Squab : See Pigeon. Can also apply to very young chickens also known as poussins.

Squash : A fleshy-fruited vegetable of which there are many varieties, and belong to the gourd section of the cucumber family, as do marrows, courgettes and pumpkins. Often bland and watery, they are mainly used for stuffing, steaming, sautéeing or baking. There are many varieties such as: acorn, spaghetti, butternut, custard, marrow, dudi, karella and many more.

Squid : (Calamari, Sleeve fish). A mollusc with a torpedo-shaped body and a transparent inner shell. It has a delicious, delicate flavour. Can be stuffed and baked, or quickly stir-fried. Usually sold already prepared, as it requires unusual treatment, similar to octopus, where only the tentacles and sac are used, the head and innards etc. being discarded. See also cuttlefish.

Stabilisers : See Emulsions.

Stag : A bull that is castrated after maturity. See also Steer.

Staling : In relation to bread, it refers to the drying out by evaporation of water content.

Star Anise : (Badian, Chinese Anise). Dried star-shaped pods, containing small oval seeds. Available as pods (whole or cracked), and whole or ground seeds. Contains the same essential oils as Anise and is one of the ingredients of 'five-spice' powder, it is used extensively in Chinese cooking. Can be substituted by Cinnamon.

Starch : Carbohydrate obtained from cereal and potatoes, which is a major source of energy.

Starch Syrup : See Glucose Syrup.

Starfish : See Actinia.

Star Fruit : Pale yellow-green and has five ribs, so when cut cross ways gives star shaped slices. Crisp and lemony. Best in fruit salads.

Steak : A thick slice of meat or fish cut from the raw flesh before any preparation.

Steam Baking : Baking in an oven with pipes through which steam passes to maintain an even temperature, and not to be confused with cooking in 'live' open steam. See Steaming.

Steaming : Cooking food in the steam rising from boiling water, by placing the food in a container with a perforated base, which is placed above a suitable vessel containing boiling water. A slower process than pure boiling.

Steeping : Soaking in liquid until saturated with a soluble ingredient, or soaking to remove an ingredient, e.g. salt from smoked ham or salt cod.

Steer : A bull that is castrated when very young. See also Stag.

Sterilising : Destroying germs or bacteria by exposing food to heat, and when immediately canned, is preserved indefinitely.

Sterlet : A small sturgeon, whose roe produces the finest golden caviar.

Stewing : To simmer food slowly on top of a cooker in a covered pan or casserole. Ideal for tough meat or vegetables.

Sticky Rice : See Glutinous Rice.

Stilton Cheese : Known generally as the King of English cheeses. Between the distinctive blue patches of mould, there should be a rich creamy colour cheese. White shows a sign of immaturity. It has a strong sometimes tangy, lingering taste. Ideal with biscuits, and not to be wasted on cooking.

Stir-Frying : A quick method of frying food in shallow fat or oil, used extensively by the Chinese. The food is cut into small even-sized pieces, and stirred constantly until cooked. Ideally cooked in a Wok, or if not available, then a round-sided frying pan.

Stirring : Mixing with a circular movement, using a spoon or fork.

Stock : Liquid that has absorbed the flavour of the fish, meat, or vegetables that have been cooked in it, or a liquid produced from slowly simmering for several hours, the offcuts of meat, fish or poultry, including the bones or carcases, with herbs and flavourings added. The stock is then used as a basis for soups, sauces, or as an ingredient for a main dish. Available in solid form as stock or boullion cubes.

Stone Ground : A term normally associated with flour which simply means that it has been ground, in the traditional way, between two large stones.

Stracchino (It.) : Soft goat cheese.

Straining : Separating liquids from solids by passing them through a metal or nylon sieve, or muslin.

Strawberries : Probably the most popular of all soft fruits. There are several varieties which vary in sweetness and redness. The sweet red juicy berries should be used on the day of purchase. Best served fresh with cream, but can be used fresh in cakes and tarts, or for making excellent jam.

Strawberry Spinach : See Swiss Chard.

Strawberry Tomato : (Coqueret). Small yellow fruit with a sweet and sour taste. Used mainly for jams and confectionary.

String Bean : See French Bean.

Strong Cheese : A savoury mixture of grated milk cheese, salt and herbs that is marinated in white wine and brandy, then allowed to ferment.

Strong Flour : Flour made from hard wheat that forms a strong elastic dough. Used mainly in bread making.

Strudel (Aus.) : Thin leaves of pastry dough, filled with fruit, nuts or savoury mixtures, which are rolled and baked.

Stuffing : Savoury mixture of bread or rice, herbs, fruit or mince meat, used to fill meat, poultry, fish or vegetables.

Sturgeon : A large seawater fish known more for its roe which produces caviar. However, it also has a well flavoured flesh, with a slight resemblance to veal.

Succotash (U.S.) : An American dish made from green corn and lima beans.

Suckling Pig : A term used to describe an unweaned pig. The flesh must be eaten as soon after killing as possible.

Sucrose : The chemical name for common sugar.

Sudare (Jap.) : Small bamboo mat used to roll sushi.

Suet : Fat around beef or lamb kidneys and loins. Used for making pastry, and normally bought in packets rather than prepared at home.

Sugar : The most common type of sweetener, correctly known as sucrose, is made from either sugar cane or sugar beet and there are numerous types, the most common being white granulated. See seperate headings of different types for descriptions and uses. No sugar, other than raw cane sugar has any nutritional value, and all are cariogenic, so should be avoided if possible, but of course, they are a necessary ingredient in many recipes.

Sugarbeet : A turnip-like vegetable grown specifically for producing sugar.

Sugar Melon : A variety of sweet juicy cantaloup, recognised by its grey ribbed skin.

Sugar Pea : See Mangetout.

Suimono (Jap.) : Clear soup.

Sukiyaki (Jap.) : Meat or vegetable dishes cooked in soy sauce, sake and sugar.

Sultanas : Dried golden sultana grapes. Sometimes known as seedless raisins.

Sumashijiru (Jap.) : Stew.

Summer Cabbage : A variety of cabbage available in summer and autumn, which has a good ball-head.

Sundae : Dessert composed of various types of ice-cream and topped with fresh fruit and cream.

Sunflower Seed : Mainly used for making cooking oil, but can be eaten raw in salads, added to casseroles, roasted, salted, or added to breads and cakes to give a crisp, nutty taste.

Sunomono (Jap.) : Salad dishes with vinegar.

Suribachi (Jap.) : See Mortar.

Sushi (Jap.) : Vinegared rice.

Sweating : Gently simmering food in a little fat or oil, until the juices start to run. A method normally reserved for vegetables.

Swede : (Rutabaga). A white-fleshed vegetable, similar to turnip but milder and sweeter, with a purplish coloured skin. An ideal addition to any stew, casserole or vegetable soup, or even a separate dish for accompanying meat or fish. Best diced or mashed, and possibly mixed with potatoes.

Swedish Anchovy : See Sprat.

Sweet : See Dessert.

Sweetbreads : Parts of the Pancreatic and Thymus gland of calves and lambs, which are considered a delicacy. Use either braised or fried, on toast. Pig's sweetbreads are not suitable to eat.

Sweetcorn : (Corn, Indian Corn). A variety of maize that is available fresh, frozen or canned. The fresh corn is bought, normally boiled and served 'on the cob' with butter, but the kernels may be scraped off after cooking and eaten separately. As its name suggests, it has a distinctive sweet flavour. See also Maize.

Sweet Herbs : A culinary term used to describe the type of herbs contained in a bouquet garni.

Sweeten : To add sugar or similar substances to a preparation, or to reduce the saltiness of a mixture by diluting with water, milk or stock.

Sweetmeat : See Candied Fruit.

Sweet Peppers : See Capsicum.

Sweet Potato : (American Yam, Batata Kumara or Long Potato). Either white or reddish-skinned vegetable, with slightly yellow sweet flesh. Can be boiled, steamed or baked either in casseroles, sweet dishes and pies, or whole in their jackets. There is normally no need to peel before use, but scrub well. A favourite in Creole cooking, where it is also used to make desserts. Do not confuse with the West Indian Yam, which despite its name, is not related to potatoes even though it is similar in appearance and uses.

Sweet Rice : See Glutinous Rice.

Sweet Sop : See Custard Apple.

Swiss Chard : (Beetleaf, Whitebeet, Seakale, Silver Chard, Strawberry Spinach and Spinach beet). A member of the *Beet* family, similar to spinach but with a stronger flavour and coarser leaves. Can be cooked and used as spinach, although it is best to remove the thick coarse stalks, and chop the midribs and leaves. Can be fried after boiling.

Swizzle Stick : Small handtool used to whisk small amounts of liquid, normally drinks or fruit juices.

Swordfish : Very large seawater fish, with fine, white delicate flesh. Prepare and cook as tuna.

Syllabub : Cold dessert of sweetened thick cream, white wine, sherry or fruit juice.

Synthetic Cream : Emulsion of vegetable oil, milk (fresh or powdered) egg yolk and sugar, or water and various synthetic materials.

Syrup : A thick sweet liquid made by boiling sugar with water and/or fruit juice.

Syrup Gum : A boiled mixture of gum arabic and sugar.

Szechuan Cabbage (Chin.) : A very hot and salty product sold in tins. Can be made from adding paprika to salted cabbage, and marinating for a few days.

Szechuan Pepper : (Anise, Chinese or Japanese Peppers). Made from the dried reddish-brown berries of the same plant, it has a hot aromatic flavour and is an ingredient of 'Five-Spice' powder. Can if necessary, be substituted by ordinary black pepper, but it is not the same.

Tabasco : A very hot sauce made from chillies, salt and vinegar. Although some dishes explicitly ask for tabasco, it is also a very good and convenient substitute for dried red chillies or chilli powder, but only a few drops are needed to flavour a dish.

Table de'hote (Fr.) : A meal of three or more courses set at a fixed price. See also A la Carte.

Table Salt : The mineral Sodium Chloride which has been extracted from underground deposits to which ingredients have been added to prevent hardening.

Tagliarini (It.) : Thin noodle strips, about a third the width of average noodles.

Tagliatelle (It.) : Thin flat egg noodles.

Tahini : An oily paste made from sesame seeds. It is sometimes added to hummus, or miso. It is highly nutritious, and is pleasant just as a spread on toast.

Takenoko (Jap.) : See Bamboo Shoot.

Talmouse : Either sweet or savoury individual soufflés.

Tamago (Jap.) : See Tofu.

Tamara (It.) : Italian curry powder made from ground aniseed, cloves, coriander seed, cinnamon and fennel.

Tamarillo : (Tree Tomato). It is a tropical fruit of the same family as the tomato, and is either reddish/yellow or purple in colour when ripe. Can be eaten raw, but is normally stewed.

Tamarind : (Indian Date). The dried fruit of the *Tamarind* Tree, it is shaped like a large broad bean with a brittle brown shell. Although it is often referred to as 'tamarind seed', it is in fact the brown pulp around the shiny dark seeds which is used in seasonings, curries and drinks, giving a sour fruity taste. When bought dried, it is soaked in hot water for 5-10 minutes until soft when it is squeezed to remove the flavour, and the seeds and fibres are then discarded and the liquid used as required. Can be substituted by vinegar.

Tamari Soy (Jap.) : A salt-free soy sauce.

Tammy : An old cooking term for straining food through a fine linen or flannel cloth. Also refers to the cloth itself.

Tandoor (Ind.) : An Indian clay oven, often buried in the ground, which produces a very high temperature. Mainly used for cooking chicken (Tandoori) and Naan bread.

Tangelo : (Mineola fruit). A hybrid fruit of a tangerine and grapefruit. Peel and prepare as for oranges. Very similar to ugli fruit.

Tangerine : A small type of sweet orange, distinguished by its loose, bright-orange red skin and small juicy segments, containing numerous pips, but makes a delicious dessert fruit. Also good for marmalade. Similar to mandarine.

Tapas (Sp.) : 'Little dishes, for picking at with drinks to sharpen the appetite for example, mushrooms in garlic sauce or chickpeas and tripe.

Tapioca : A starch food prepared from the root of the *Cassava or Manioc* plant. The resultant paste is heated to burst the granules, which are then dried and left in globules, like sago, or flaked. Used to thicken stews or soups, and for making milk puddings.

Taro : See Eddoe.

Tarragon : (Estragon) A strong distinctive fresh anise flavoured herb, the leaves are used either fresh on salads, or for certain egg or cheese dishes, or in a vinegar form to enhance a sauce such as Tartare. Should be used sparingly. Also available as whole dried leaves or powdered. Ideal with Mushrooms.

Tart : (Pie). Similar to a flan, but refers to a pastry case filled with either a fruit or custard, with or without a pastry top. See also Flan Pie and Open Tart.

Tartare : Cold mayonnaise sauce made from hard-boiled egg yolks, olive oil and chives.

Tartaric Acid : An acid that is present in many fruits. The extracted acid is used in the manufacture of mineral and effervescent drinks.

Tartlet : Small tart.

Taste : In general terms, the initial flavour of a single item of food, or the resultant effect on the palate of a mixture of various flavours.

Tatami (Jap.) : Matting woven from rice straw.

Tea : Universal beverage made from the infused leaves of the *Thea Sinensis* tree. Tea can vary immensely according to the treatment of the leaves during the drying process.

Teal : The most common wild duck with short pointed feathers and thin soft feet. Does not normally need hanging. Excellent for roasting or grilling. Allow one bird per person.

Teff : See Millet.

Tempeh : Fermented soya bean. Available as a densely packed cake and can be used in stir-fries and soups. Can be used as an excellent substitute for tofu.

Tempura (Jap.) : Any ingredient dipped in batter and deep-fried in oil, similar to fritters.

Tench : A freshwater fish similar to a small carp. To remove scales, place fish in boiling water to scald.

Tenderising : Beating raw meat with a spiked mallet or rolling pin to soften the meat, usually steaks, prior to grilling or frying. Also means the addition of a tenderiser such as vinegar or lemon juice.

Tenderloin (U.S.) : See Beef Fillet.

Tendon : The gristly cord which connects the various muscle formations in animals, and should be removed during preparation.

Tepid : See Lukewarm.

Teriyaki (Jap.) : Fish marinated in a sauce and broiled.

Terrapin : A small, land-based variety of turtle. The flesh is not as succulent as the water turtle.

Terrine (Fr.) : Pâté or minced mixture baked or steamed in a loaf tin or earthenware container.

Texturised Vegetable Protein : Commonly known as TVP. It is a meat substitute made from vegetables, usually soya beans, which absorbs the flavour of the ingredients it is cooked in.

Thickening : A mixture such as flour and butter, egg yolk, or cream, used to thicken, bind and give body to sauces and soups.

Thick Soups : A stock or consommé, to which various ingredients have been added that naturally thicken the stock, and/or the addition of a roux, egg yolks or cream as liaison agents. Thick soups are often puréed or creamed.

Thistle : Species of wild plant which includes artichokes and cardoons.

Thonine : Mediterranean species of tuna fish.

Thonné : A method of cooking veal, which is first marinated in oil, thyme, bay leaf, lemon juice and spices.

Thyme : A strong pungent herb available as fresh or dried leaves, used mainly in stuffings for meat and poultry or to flavour vegetables such as potatoes, tomatoes, courgettes and aubergines. Also an ingredient of bouquet garnis. See also Lemon Thyme.

Tigernut : (Chufa nuts). Although always referred to as nuts, they are in fact the rhizomes of a plant. Usually sold dried, they have an almondy taste and can be eaten on their own like peanuts. Sometimes available ground.

Tilsit Cheese (Ger.) : A savoury straw-coloured slicing cheese, easily recognisable by its loaf shape and small irregular holes. It has a sharp, slightly sour taste.

Timbale (Fr.) : Cup-shaped earthenware or metal mould, or food cooked in such a mould.

Tiramsu (It.) : Italian dessert made with Marsala and Mascapone.

Toast : Bread that is grilled, dry, until golden brown.

Toasted Sesame Oil : A strong nutty flavoured oil, extracted from toasted sesame seeds, which is only used in small doses for its aromatic qualities, and not as a cooking medium. A mere half teaspoon is needed to flavour a whole bowl of salad. Do not confuse with ordinary sesame oil.

Toddy : A name for a type of rum punch, often served hot.

Toffee : Sweetmeat made from fat, milk, sugar and confectionary glucose. Similar to but harder than caramel.

Tofu : A white bean curd made from soya beans, which has the protein equivalent of eggs. The smoked variety has a subtle flavour, but the plain white variety is completely tasteless. A reasonable substitute for eggs in lacto and vegan dishes.

Tomato : One of the most common and versatile of vegetables. The small 'home-grown' products are by far the best for using raw - there is nothing tastier than a freshly picked tomato. The larger squat varieties are more suitable for stuffing and grilling or frying. All types should be firm and regular in shape, and bright in colour, with a matt-textured skin. Avoid any with blotched or cracked skins.

Tome Au Raisin (Fr.) : A white, slightly chewy strong-flavoured cheese covered in dry black grape pips.

Tome De Savoie (Fr.) : A semi-hard yellow, strong-flavoured cheese with a reddish rind.

Tongs : An instrument with two sprung various-shaped prongs, used to lift food items during both cooking and serving at table.

Tongue : Ox and lamb's tongues are the most readily available. Calf's tongue is rare, and pig's tongue is always sold with the head. Lamb's tongue is small, weighing about 8 oz. It should be soaked in lightly salted water before boiling or braising. Ox tongue weighs about 4-6 lbs. and can be purchased fresh or salted. It must be slowly boiled for several hours, and the rough skin removed before serving.

Tongue Cress : See Watercress.

Tonka Bean : A seed pod with similar characteristics to vanilla pods, but a lower quality.

Top Fruit : The term used for all tree fruits such as apples and pears, and also stoned fruits, such as cherries, peaches, plums and nuts. Eat as near to day of purchase as possible, as most do not store well.

Torbay Sole : See Witch. Do not confuse with Sole.

Torte (Fr.) : A term used to describe both sweet and savoury dishes that are round in shape.

Tortilla : Large flat pancake made from ground Maize, corn or wholewheat. They freeze well.

Toso (Jap.) : A good quality Sake.

Tot : Name given to a small measure of spirits.

Tournedo : Small round slices of beef fillet sautéed in butter or grilled and basted in butter.

Toxins : A potentially harmful substance if taken in anything but very small doses - there are minor traces of the substance in most foods, and generally cause no problems. However, most of the kidney bean family have a toxin in their skins which must be destroyed by fast-boiling for 10 minutes and throwing the water away. Never cook beans in a slow cooker and never attempt to eat them raw.

Transparent Noodles (Chin.) Clear variety of noodles that must be well soaked before cooking. Used in stir-fry or slow-cook dishes, and are ideal for absorbing the liquids and flavours of the other ingredients. Normally sold in bundles. See also Cellophane Noodles.

Trappistenkäse Cheese (Ger.) : Pale yellow semi-soft cheese with a mild flavour and a rich yellow rind, made in loaves or bars. It has a firm consistency with round or slotted eyes.

Treacle : The first product of refining molasses from sugar beet or cane. A dark brown semi-liquid, the consistency of honey, which will not crystallise. Mainly used in confectionary, puddings and cakes or bread.

Tree-Fungi (Chin.) : (Wood-Ears). A fungi, greyish in colour, with a slippery yet crunchy texture, used mainly in stir-fry dishes.

Tree Tomato : See Tamarillo.

Tree Onion : See Rocambole.

Trepang : See Bech-de-Mer.

Trifle : A dessert made from layers of sponge cake, soaked in wine, liqueur or fruit juice, and spread with cream, custard, nuts and cherries.

Trigger Fish : (Pigfish). Fairly small fish with medium quality flesh. Cook as tuna.

Trim : To remove unwanted, inedible parts of food, or to improve its appearance by shaping.

Tripe : The lining of an ox stomach. The lining from the first stomach is the finest and smoothest, and known as Blanket. The second stomach produces Honeymoon Tripe. Both types should be thick, firm and white; avoid any that is slimy and grey, or has a flabby appearance. Normally sold partly boiled. Can be boiled, stewed or deep-fried.

Triticale : A hybrid seed sprout of wheat and rye, which is used as bean sprouts. Very rich in protein.

Trivet : A rock used in the oven or pan to hold the meat away from the direct heat to prevent excessive evaporation.

Trout : A readily available slightly oily fish, ideal for grilling or poaching, normally cooked whole. Also sold smoked. See Rainbow, River, Salmon, Sea and Smoked Trout for varieties.

Truffles : Rare mushroom-like fungus that grows underground, black or white in colour, with a firm texture and delicate taste. Expensive delicacies, and mainly used for garnishing, or larding.

Trussed/Trussing : Tying a bird after it has been dressed to secure the legs and wings or joint of meat, to keep it in a neat shape with skewers and/or string before cooking.

Tube-Pan : Ring-shaped tin for baking cakes.

Tuber : The edible underground food storage organ of some plants, like Potato or Yam.

Tuna : (Germon, Tunny). A very versatile and popular oily, fatty firm-fleshed fish, which can be eaten either fresh, salted, smoked or is very commonly purchased tinned in brine or oil.

Tunny : See Tuna.

Turban Shell : See Acorn Barnacle.

Turbot : An exquisitely flavoured flat fish with firm, meaty flesh, normally bought as steaks or fillets, and can be grilled, sautéed or poached. Young, or 'chicken' turbot is best cooked whole on the bone. The head, skin and bones are excellent for fish stocks and sauces.

Turbot Sole : See Witch. Do not confuse with either Turbot or Sole.

Tureen : A wide, deep dish from which soup or stew is cooked, and often served at table.

Turkey : A poultry bird, varying in size from 6-40 lbs., with a stronger flavour than chicken, and treated in the same way for cooking, especially hen-birds, being about 8-10 lbs, the larger cock birds being normally only roasted whole, in foil, due to their size.

Turmeric : (Haldi). A strong pleasantly bitter earthy spice with a rich golden yellow colour, which is a rhizome or root stem of the *Ginger* family, available dried whole or ground. It is used mainly for colouring Eastern dishes, both meat, fish and rice. Can be a substitute for saffron to add a similar colour only, the fragrance being completely different. Use sparingly and be careful when using, as it easily stains clothes and even work surfaces.

Turnip : An ideal root vegetable for stews or casseroles. The skin is yellowish and fairly thick, and should be peeled before cooking. The flesh is white to yellow and easily absorbs fats and juices, making it a good vegetable for roasts.

Turnover : A sweet dessert made by folding a circle or square of flaky pastry in half over a filling to form a semi-circle or triangle and then baked. A savoury version is known as a pasty.

Turtle : A hard-shelled water reptile, whose succulent and uniquely flavoured flesh is most commonly used to make soup.

Tutti Frutti (It.) : Dried or candied mixed, added to ice cream.

T V P : A common abbreviation for Textured Vegetable Protein.

Tzatziki : A Greek dip made of yoghurt, cucumber, mint and garlic.

𝒰

Udon (Jap.) : Broad wheat flour noodles. Can be substituted by spaghetti.

Ugli Fruit : A hybrid citrus fruit, being a cross between a tangerine and a grapefruit. It is similar to a grapefruit in appearance, except that its skin is thick, knobbly and greenish-yellow. Its sweet pink flesh can be eaten raw, or used in preserves, or baked. See Tangelo.

Ukha (Russ.) : Describes any Russian fish soup.

Ulva (Jap.) : Variety of edible seaweed.

Ullage : The liquid remains of a damaged cask or bottle.

Umbles : Edible entrails of animals. Used as the main ingredient of 'Humble Pie', hence the saying.

Umbra /Umbrine : Seawater fish resembling and cooked as bass.

Umeboshi Plums (Jap.) : Japanese salted and pickled plums that are available whole or puréed, and are used as a flavouring in savoury drinks and vinegar. The puréed plums and vinegar can be used in stir-fry dishes. The whole plums can be boiled with rice, or sliced and added to vegetables.

Unagi (Jap.) : See Eel.

Uni (Jap.) : See Sea-urchin.

Unleavened Bread: Bread made without a raising agent which, when baked, is thin, flat and round.

Unrefined : An item of food in a natural, non-processed state, as with raw cane sugar and whole grain.

Unsaturated Margarine : The soft variety of margarine, that contains a lower proportion of saturated fats, but a higher percentage of water than the 'solid' variety.

Urd Bean : (Black Gram). Similar in appearance to mung beans, they are available whole or split and skinless. Treat as other legumes.

Urhad Dal (Ind.) : Indian pulses often sold as lentils. Ground urhad dal is used to make poppadoms.

Vacherin Cheese : A round, semi-soft, off-white cheese with a rough, mottled rind, and a mild flavour.

Valencay/Levroux Cheese : Square-shaped, soft, full-flavoured creamy goat cheese with a grey edible crust.

Valencia : A round, thin-skinned orange, with sweet very juicy flesh, and practically pipless.

Vanilla : A flavouring commonly sold as an essence, made from vanilla pods which are the dried fruits of an *Orchid* plant, and are at their best when dark brown, flexible and covered with a frosting of aromatic vanillin crystals. The pods can be re-used about ten times if washed and dried and then buried in sugar after use each time. The flavouring is used in all forms of confectionary, the most well-known form being vanilla ice cream.

Vanilla Sugar : Sugar flavoured with vanilla by enclosing it with a vanilla pod in a closed jar.

Varak : See Silver Leaf.

Variety Meat : American term for offal.

Veal : The meat of a calf, the young of a cow, which is only three months old and fed exclusively on milk. Should have white non-greasy flesh, and probably the most delicately flavoured variety of meat.

Vegan : The ultimate ethical diet that avoids all animal foods - including eggs and dairy produce. It consists basically of vegetables, grains, nuts, seeds, seaweeds, fresh and dried fruits.

Vegetable : Plant or part of a plant (excluding fruit), that is grown for food, and provide the most readily available source of all the essential dietary requirements of proteins, carbohydrates, fats, salts and vitamins. High in vitamin C.

Vegetable Butter : Made from naturally occurring fats, like cocoa butter.

Vegetable Gelatine : See Agar Agar.

Vegetable Pear : See Chayotte.

Vegetable Shortening : A mixture of partially hardened vegetable fats. See Lard Shortening.

Vegetable Stock : Stock made from vegetables. See Stock.

Vegetarian Cheese : Made with plant rennet, and is available in hard and soft forms which can be used in exactly the same way as cheddar or ricotta. The most common that is currently available is Galium Velum, popularly known as Lady's Bedstraw.

Velouté (Fr.) : Basic white sauce made with chicken or veal stock, or soup made with velouté sauce, rubbed through a sieve and thickened with egg yolk, cream and butter to give a creamy consistency.

Venison : A game meat, the best of which comes from the young male deer (buck). The lean dark red meat is close-grained, with firm white fat. Should be hung for at least one week. Suitable for roasting or braising. The meat toughens on animals over one year old.

Venus : See Cockle.

Verdi (It.) : Green pastas made from spinach e.g. lasagne verdi.

Verjuice : Acidic juice of unripe grapes used as vinegar.

Vermicelli (It.) : Long, fine, semi-transparent, round strands of pasta, made from mungbean flour. Normally used in soups or braised dishes. Snowy white rice vermicelli is soft and subtle in taste, and used extensively in Asian dishes and desserts.

Vermouth : A variety of dry or white wines that have been infused with herbs. Used in many culinary dishes and cocktails as a mixer.

Veronique (Fr.) : Denotes the use of grapes in a dish.

Vetch : A group of sprawling bushy plants, which produce pulses such as asparagus peas, which are eaten while still green.

Vichysoisse (Fr.) : Chilled leek and potato soup.

Vierge : A beaten mixture of butter, salt, pepper and lemon juice, and served with vegetables.

Vinaigrette : Mixture of oil, vinegar, salt and pepper, which is sometimes flavoured with chopped herbs.

Vinegar : A clear liquid, although often tinted with caramel, consisting mainly of acetic acid, obtained by the fermentation of wine, cider or malt beer. Used mainly to pickle or preserve foodstuffs. A multitude of flavoured Cider Vinegars are available as condiments.

Vine Leaves : (Grape leaves). Used as a wrapping to form a parcel of food in many Middle Eastern dishes, as in dolmades, but can also be fried in batter or cut up and added to salads.

Vitamins : These substances of which there are about 13 types are necessary to ensure a healthy body. They fall into two main categories. The first is water-soluble, such as vitamins B, C and folic acid. These cannot be stored in the body for long periods, and are also easily lost in cooking, so a regular daily intake is required. The other category is fat-soluble vitamins such as A, D, E, and K which are stored by the body in the liver and fatty tissues, and therefore need not be consumed in daily amounts, and are easier to retain in foods as they are more stable in cooking and processing.

Vitellin : The main protein in egg yolks.

Vol-Au-Vent (Fr.) : An entrée consisting of a light flaky case of puff pastry with a lid, filled with a savoury mixture of diced meat, poultry, fish or vegetables after cooking. Often included in a buffet meal.

Wafer : Thin biscuit made with rice flour and served with ice cream or mousse desserts.

Waffle : (Hotbreads). Batter cooked in a hot buttered waffle iron to a crisp biscuit. See Fritters.

Wakame (Jap.) : A versatile variety of seaweed with long, thin curly ribbon-like strands. Used in soups, stocks or salads. Can also be soaked and cut into strips for wrapping up pieces of raw fish and then fried. Also available shredded, in a ready-to-eat form.

Waldorf Salad : Salad with apples, walnuts, celery, sultanas and mayonniase.

Walnut : A very versatile nut with many varieties, which is sold either whole, shelled, ground and chopped, dried or pickled. They are used at various stages of their growth for different types of recipes. The moister the walnut, the fresher, or younger it is. Green walnuts, which have not yet developed a hard shell, are picked to make pickles, ketchups and chutneys. Wet walnuts have moist kernels but with a hard outer shell. They have a delicious, fragrant flavour, and are marvellous in savoury dishes. Dried walnuts, the type most often eaten, are simply the version of wet nuts from which the moisture has been allowed to evaporate, and are either eaten whole as a snack, or added to salads, cakes and breads.

Walnut Oil : Made from cold pressed ripe nuts, and makes a subtle salad dressing.

Warabe (Jap.) : Edible bracken or fern shoots.

Wasabi (Jap.) : (Japanese Horseradish). A hot green variety of horseradish. Available fresh, tinned or in jars and tubes. Useful for dishes that need an extra strong sharp pungency. Can be substituted by English mustard.

Water Chestnut : (Caltropes). A large crunchy, walnut-sized bulb with brown skin and a tasty white crisp flesh that can be eaten raw or roasted. Available either fresh or canned, ready peeled.

Watercress : (Tongue or Garden Cress). A small dark green leafy plant whose raw sprigs are used to garnish meat or fish dishes, as a salad ingredient or part of a sandwich filling. See also Landcress. Keeps for only 2 days.

Water Melon : A variety of melon that has a dark green skin and pinkish flesh, with a very 'watery' consistency, and rather insipid taste.

Wax Bean (U.S.) : (Yellow Wax Bean). An American variety of Green Bean.

Wax Gourd : A variety of gourd that is a member of the marrow and squash family.

Well : A hollow or dip made in pile or bowlful of flour into which other ingredients are placed before mixing.

Welsh Onion : (Cibol, Japanese Bunching Onion). An evergreen plant which produces clumps of hollow leaves up to 2 feet tall, with fleshy, sweet bases, and are used as a substitute for spring onions. Very high in vitamin C.

Welsh Rabbit : (Rarebit). A snack made from melted cheese mixed with mustard, spread on buttered toast, and then grilled.

Wensleydale Cheese : A mild-flavoured, crumbly cheese, which varies in colour from white to creamy-yellow. Ideal for cooking.

West Indian Cherry : (Acerola, Antilles, Barbados or Malpighia Cherry). The fruit of the small, bushy *Malpighia* tree. The richest known source of vitamin C.

West Indian Yam : See Yam.

Wether : Name for a castrated ram.

Whale Meat : A popular Japanese ingredient, with a unique flavour between fish and beef.

Wheat : Probably the most important grain of all, even more than rice. There are two basic types; Common or Bread Wheat for making flour to be used in breads and cakes. The hard grained varieties for bread making, and the soft grained varieties for cakes, desserts and sauces, and Durum Wheat which is used for making semolina. Most of them are very high in gluten, which is necessary for bread-making and baking. Wheat is available in many forms, such as cracked, flaked or floured. See individual types of flours for descriptions and uses.

Wheat Flakes : Are flattened grains which are normally toasted. They can be eaten raw as part of a breakfast cereal or cooked, like rolled oats and made into a course porridge. Wheat bran or germ can also be used as cereals.

Wheat Flour : Available in many different forms such as granary, plain/all-purpose, self-raising, matzoh, wholemeal etc.. See individual headings for descriptions and uses.

Wheat Flour Of 81% Extraction : (Wheatmeal). The grain has up to 20% of its coarser elements removed during milling, which then makes good tasty loaves, or thickens soups or stews without making them gritty or stodgy.

Wheatmeal : Now known as Wheat Flour of 81% extraction.

Whelks : They have a snail-like shell, and can be eaten raw, but are normally lightly boiled, as they become very tough if overcooked. Tasty when eaten with vinegar. Also good for flavouring soups and sauces.

Whey : Liquid which separates from the curd when milk curdles. Used in cheese-making.

Whey Cheese : Made from whey by heating, which causes coagulation of the proteins.

Whipping : Beating eggs until frothy, or cream until thick and 'peaky'.

Whisk : Looped wire utensil used to beat air into eggs, cream or batters.

Whisking : As whipping.

Whitebait : The fry or young of the herring or sprat, about 25mm long, silvery skinned with firm grey-white flesh. Normally deep-fried, and eaten whole. Delicious as a snack on toast.

White Beet : Variety of chard.

White Cabbage : A white-leaved winter cabbage which is excellent for storage, or making coleslaw or sauerkraut.

White Currants : Identical in size and shape to red currants, but only used as a dessert fruit with sugar.

White Fish : This term describes fish where oil is only found in the liver, such as cod, halibut, haddock and plaice, whereas oily fish have oil throughout the whole flesh. The produce **must** be absolutely fresh, which can be recognised by its firm, even-textured flesh, clear, full shiny eyes, and bright red gills and a clean sea smell. Steaks, cutlets and fillets, should have firm closely packed flakes and no 'watery' look.

White Pepper : Has the same uses as black pepper, but is less pungent and aromatic.

White Salmon : See Bass.

Whiting : (Silver Hake). A cheap member of the cod family, and always readily available. The flesh tends to be on the dry side, with delicate white flakes and so is not recommended for grilling, but is suitable for most recipes for white fish.

Wholemeal Corn : A variety of corn grain that has a low gluten content, so it will not leaven bread, but can be used ground to sprinkle over bread before baking, or scattered on the greased surfaces of tins or baking sheets to aid removal after cooking.

Wholemeal Flour : The British name given to any flour made from the whole grain, which is often confused with wholewheat flour. Fortunately, the term 'wholemeal' is gradually becoming extinct.

Wholewheat Flour : This flour is coarse in texture and brown in colour, as it contains all the bran and wheatgerm, and because of this, it makes a delicious if somewhat densely-textured bread, but its fibre content is particularly valuable. Some makes are labelled 'Stoneground', which simply means that it has been ground in the traditional way, between two large stones. See also Graham Flour.

Whortleberry : See Bilberry.

Widgeon : A small bird, similar to and cooked as wild duck or mallard.

Wiener Schnitzel (Aus.) : Veal slice cooked in the Viennese style, e.g. coated in egg and breadcrumbs, fried in butter and garnished with anchovies and capers.

Wild Boar : A mammal similar to a pig. The meat can only really be eaten from animals less than six months old, after which time only the head is really edible. In all cases, the meat should be well marinated before cooking.

Wild Chervil : (Cecily). Similar to cultivated chervil, but has a much more bitter flavour.

Wild Chicory : Slightly bitter but pleasant form of chicory, with tender leaves used in salads.

Wild Duck : See Mallard.

Wild Marjoram : (Organt). Similar to marjoram, but has a pungent smell and bitter taste.

Wildrice : (Zizanie). Despite its name, this is not really rice, but a wild grass which, when cooked in the same way as rice, has a pleasant nutty flavour, and makes a good alternative to ordinary rice in savoury dishes. It can be expensive.

Wild Spinach : See Good King Henry.

William Pear : Large, sweet, juicy variety of dessert pear.

Windberry : See Bilberry.

Windsor Bean : See Broad Bean.

Wine : Normally fermented grape juice, but can also be made from vegetables or other fruit juices.

Wine Sediment Paste (Chin.) : A difficult product to purchase in the West, but satisfactory substitute recipes can be found in most good Chinese cookery books. It is used mainly in the preparation of cold dishes and gives a similar flavour to 'smoked' meats, fish etc.

Winged Pea : See Asparagus Pea.

Winkles : (Periwinkles) A small, black snail-shelled mollusc, with a fresh salty tang. They are cooked by lightly boiling, similar to cockles. They are normally removed from their shells by using a pin or similar object.

Winter Artichoke : See Artichoke Jerusalem.

Winter Cabbage : A type of cabbage that matures in the winter, generally ball or drum headed, with green or white varieties which store well.

Winter Cauliflower : A term used to describe the white headed vegetable available during late winter and spring, but it is in fact a heading broccoli which forms a single white head, and is less delicately flavoured than true cauliflower, of which there is no winter variety.

Winter Cress : (Barbarea). Similar to cress in taste and has the same properties.

Witch : (Torbay Sole or Turbot Sole). Do not confuse it with either turbot or sole, although it is a tasty fish, and can be used in most flat fish recipes such as plaice.

Witloof : See Chicory.

Wok : A round Chinese frying pan used for stir-frying. The food is cooked in the base area, and then spooned onto the side of the utensil to drain of oil but still remain hot.

Wolf Fish : See Catfish.

Wonton (Chin.) : (Wonton Paste, Wonton skin). Thin sheet of paste used for holding savoury fillings. Available from Chinese stores.

Woodcock : A game bird, slightly larger than snipe, being about 12oz. Considered to be the best winged game bird. Hang for 3 days and roast undrawn.

Wood Ear (Chin.) : (Cloud Ear or Wood fungus). A dried black fungus which should be soaked for 20 minutes before use, or until they become glutinous and crinkly.

Wood Fungus : See Wood Ear.

Wood Grouse : See Grouse.

Wood Pigeon : See pigeon.

Worcester Sauce : The Brand name of a hottish sauce which contains anchovies. Can be useful as an extra flavouring in some sauces, soups and stews, added to raw avocado pears or sprinkled over steaks or chops. It is also tasty when added to tomato juice in a cocktail.

Wrasse : An uncommon bony fish, considered a delicacy in some countries. It has a good flavour, and would be ideal for stocks, soups and sauces.

Wrinkled Peas : (Marrowfat Peas). A variety of green pea that is sweeter and larger than the round varieties, and readily available fresh in the summer. Also available dried, frozen or tinned.

Xavier : A clear soup served with cheese quenelles.
Xeres (Spn.) : A dark, full flavoured Spanish sherry.

Yakidofu (Jap.) : Broiled soybean curd.
Yakimono (Jap.) : A general term for broiling.
Yakitori (Jap.) : Broiled chicken.
Yakumi (Jap.) : Garnish.
Yam : (West Indian Yam). A large sweet tuberous root with orange, moist, oily textured flesh. Not to be confused with the American yam which is simply another name for Sweet Potato. These West Indian yams have a thick outer skin or bark which must be peeled off before cooking. They can be boiled, roasted, mashed or fried, and have the same uses as ordinary potatoes.
Yamaimo (Jap.) : Japanese Yam.
Yarmouth Bloater : See Red Herring.
Yeast : Fungus cells used to produce alcoholic fermentation, or to cause dough to rise. Can be bought fresh, and will last two weeks if wrapped in a refrigerator, or dried in a powder form for convenience.
Yeast Extracts : Used mainly as sandwich spreads, or made into hot savoury drinks by just adding boiling water, or added to soups or stews as a flavouring in place of boullion cubes. They are very nutritious.
Yell Flounder (U.S.) : See Lemon Sole.
Yellow Wax Bean : See Wax Bean.

Yoghurt : Most common form of curdled milk i.e. milk which has been treated and thickened with harmless bacteria and yeast. In the Middle East it is served as a sauce with meat, fish and vegetables. In Europe it is mainly served with or in desserts.

Yorkshire Pudding : Thick type of batter pancake, generally eaten as an accompaniment to roast beef dishes.

Yuzu (Jap.) : Lemon or Lime.

Zabaglione (It.) : Dessert cream mousse, consisting of egg yolks, white wine or marsala and sugar, which are whisked together in the top of a double boiler over boiling water until thick and foamy.

Zakuski (Russ.) : Russian hors d'oeuvres, normally served to accompany vodka.

Zanda : A firm, white-fleshed fish of the pike family. Can be cooked as, and substituted for cod.

Zest : (Epicarp or Flavido). The coloured oily outer skin of citrus fruit which contains essential oil, and when grated or peeled, is used to flavour foods and liquids.

Zester : Small tool for scraping off zest of fruit.

Zitoni (It.) : A very large unfluted macaroni.

Zizanie : Another name for Wild Rice.

Zoolak : Fermented milk, similar to yoghurt.

Zucchini : A member of the gourd family, and is the most popular variety of courgette. See also Courgette.

Other cookery titles from Summersdale:

Man About The Kitchen
Alastair Williams
This cookbook is designed for men of all ages and in all situations. Topics include basic cooking skills, choosing food, delicious simple recipes, understanding wine, and dishes for special occasions. An ideal gift for any man.
£9.99

The Student Grub Guide
Alastair Williams
The bestselling student cookery book that contains a wide range of popular and easy to prepare recipes. The style is laid-back, the instructions are witty and user-friendly, and the food is delicious.
£4.99

The Vegetarian Student Grub Guide
Alastair Williams
The complete guide to vegetarian cooking for students, including an introduction to cooking techniques.
£4.99

Cooking in the Nude - Quickies
Stephen and Debbie Cornwell
A collection of elegant but easy recipes that will satisfy more than your appetite!
£6.99

Cooking in the Nude - Red Hot Lovers
Stephen and Debbie Cornwell
Spicy recipes for lovers!
£6.99

Food as Foreplay - Recipes for Romance, Love and Lust
The Cooking Couple
As seen on TV! The Cooking Couple shows you how to turn your life into a romantic feast of love, lust and happiness.
£8.99

Victorian Recipe Secrets
Rae Katherine Eighmey
Return to the 19th century for a taste of Victoriana. This cookbook includes fascinating historical notes on the origins of the recipes.
£6.99